SYM SCOTT

The Perfect Kiss
50 Ways to Kiss Your Lover

Tobacco Road Press

First published by Tobacco Road Press 2022

Copyright © 2022 by Sym Scott

Special thanks to:

Editor: Get Out My Red Pen Editing

XOXO to Kissing Coaches: Lee Loveletter, Vincent Valentino, Sultry Salbato, Ravishing Rose, Lou Losthersenses, and Babsalicious

Appreciation and Affection for Apex Authors

First edition

ISBN: 978-0-9858955-5-6

This book was professionally typeset on Reedsy. Find out more at reedsy.com

Contents

Introduction

Kissing is magic that makes time standstill.

Yet, kissing has become a lost art.

With no formal "how-to" training, most of us are on our own to figure out love, romance, and sex. We create our skill sets on trial and error rather than specific instruction and mature relationship building. Unfortunately, honest information and healthy examples are hard to find within a society that focuses on two extremes—either clean-cut piety or perfecting booty bodies over good character, caring hearts, and factual knowledge.

So here's the truth of it: **Intimacy matters**. Being a great lover *requires* that you like, respect, and enjoy the other person's company. Being interested *rather than interesting* is a form of courting and foreplay—it comes first, whether giving one fabulous New Year's Eve kiss or a lunchtime smooch after many years of marriage. Focusing on and caring about your love interest is *vital* if your intention is to engage in a worthwhile conversation, casual sex, or a long, joyful life together.

Once you've got this concept down, you'll now want to have some back-pocket kisses ready. Continue with kisses you know how to do, but don't be afraid to try something new.

Within this fun, instructional (and often steamy) relationship guidebook, you'll find a bit of everything—from sweet, small kisses (see #44) to self-worth and intimacy exploration (see #21) to off-the-charts, mind-numbing lip-locks (#38), all in the form of kissing and perhaps, *just a bit more.*

I say, let's bring the art of kissing back and spend time perfecting it. I suggest reading the kisses aloud with your partner, trying one kiss a day for ten days, and continuing if you find it beneficial. If you don't have a partner right now, prepare for one. Something magical may happen.

Consent Matters

Touch of any kind requires consent between parties. Kissing is no exception. Let's be clear that with every kiss in this series, **I'm only talking about doing it with someone who poses no threat, only safety.** Here are some excellent guidelines and reminders from *Healthline.com:

- Consent can be withdrawn at any time, even if you've already started getting intimate. All sexual activity must stop when consent is withdrawn.
- Being in a relationship doesn't oblige anyone to do anything. Consent should never be implied or assumed, even if you're in a relationship or have had sex before.
- You don't have consent if you use guilt, intimidation, or threats to coerce someone into sex, even if that person says "yes." Saying yes out of fear is not consent.
- Silence or a lack of a response is not consent.
- Be clear and concise when getting consent. Consenting to go back to your place doesn't mean they're consenting to sexual activity.
- If you're initiating sex with someone who's under the

influence of drugs or alcohol, you're responsible for obtaining ongoing, clear consent. If someone is stumbling or can't stand without leaning on someone or something, slurring their words, falling asleep, or has vomited, they're incapacitated and cannot consent.

- There's no consent when you use your power, trust, or authority to coerce someone into sex.

*https://www.healthline.com/health/guide-to-consent#guidelines-for-consent

For more on consent, please see the RAINN site @ https://www.rainn.org/articles/what-is-consent

RAINN (Rape, Abuse & Incest National Network) is the nation's largest anti-sexual violence organization. RAINN created and operates the National Sexual Assault Hotline (800.656.HOPE, **online.rainn.org** y **rainn.org/es**) in partnership with more than 1,000 local sexual assault service providers across the country and operates the DoD Safe Helpline for the Department of Defense. RAINN also carries out programs to prevent sexual violence, help survivors, and ensure perpetrators are brought to justice.

Kissing Courtesies, Clarifications, & Considerations

Kissing Courtesies

1. **Hygiene**: Do your partner (and the world) a favor by maintaining good hygiene! It's essential that your breath, body, and clothes smell fresh or neutral. If you don't already have them, create doable regimens and daily habits for brushing and flossing your teeth. Flossing is one of the best ways to maintain good breath.

2. **Chapped Lips**: If you're prone to chapped lips like I am: 1) hydrate more. Drink at least half your body weight in ounces every day for a week. Do your lips feel smoother? 2) Find a lip balm that truly works for you. While most are a temporary fix, I recently discovered one that seems to heal and maintain smooth lips for longer. I picked up a lip balm with Manuka honey when checking out at a store one day, not thinking it was anything but another lip balm. Weirdly, I woke up the next day with smooth lips,

which doesn't usually happen. As I continue to use it, my lips feel healthy and "maintained," rather than *needing* to apply lip balm all of the time.

3. **Stubble**: Keep your hair (face, privates, or legs) one of two ways: 1) smooth or 2) the hair long enough to be soft to the touch. A particular problem can be facial stubble. Not only is the sharpness of stubble *unpleasant* since it can actually hurt by tearing up the Receiver's lips and face, but it's also a *distraction* for the Receiver who is just trying to enjoy the kiss. Check-in with your person of affection (poa). Another challenge can be, shall we say, the *aroma* of the beard. If the beard-wearer smokes, a stench can build up, so this must be addressed unless the poa can't smell it or doesn't have a problem with it.

4. **Kissing Heights**: If you and your partner's heights vary quite a bit, switch it up by having the shorter one stand on steps when convenient to equalize the situation, or so that they can be taller sometimes. This saves your necks and also allows dominant roles to be reversed.

5. **Kissing requires kindness and respect**: Be present and sincere. Match the energy of your partner when approaching them romantically. Please see the chapter on "Consent."

Kissing Clarifications

***All* kisses in this book are for EVERYONE!**

Pronouns:

I use neutral pronouns such as "they," themselves," and "themself" **except** when I am telling my own stories (I know the preferred pronouns in these cases) or other people's kiss stories told to me with the pronouns they wanted to be used.

Roles:

- **The Lead:** This is the person who initiates the kiss.
- **The Receiver**: This person receives the kiss that the Lead initiated.

I identify roles similarly to partner dancing, where there is a Lead and a *Follower* except:

- ...for these *50 Kisses*, I identify a Lead and a *Receiver*.
- Once the kiss is initiated for many of the kisses, it ceases to become a Lead and Receiver situation. Both are participating equally.
- For many other kisses, the Lead and Receiver roles continue throughout.
- The roles can be reversed any time you see fit to do so.

poa - your "person of affection." This is your kissing partner.

French Kissing Toolbox - these are add-on kisses that can't be done without "French Kissing."

Kisses with Quotation Marks: These are kisses that have their own chapter and description in this *50 Kisses* book.

Video Suggestions: I make suggestions for online videos or GIFS to look up. I don't add specific URLs because videos come and go; I can't guarantee the link will still be good. And then there's copyright infringement. I don't want any problems there. Still, *seeing* makes for a better understanding. So I hope you can find the videos I'm describing.

Kissing Considerations

Intimate Kissing: When it comes to kissing, it ultimately comes down to two things: *tongue* or *no tongue*.

- **No Tongue:** This kiss can be sexual or not sexual, depending on who you're kissing. If it is a family member or friend, this is a non-sexual kiss. It's usually a hello, goodbye, or thank you sort of kiss. If it is a lover, it holds a different meaning altogether, and the "No Tongue" kiss becomes sexual, even if only short and sweet. It's what I will call a "Stage One" type of kiss.
- **Tongue**: Once the mouth opens and more exploration begins, whether, on the mouth or any other part of the body, there is no mistaking the intention. A new level of sexuality has been activated. It's a "Stage Two" type of kiss.

Non-Intimates (friends, family, and acquaintances): It can be awkward when kissing family members and platonic friends until a routine or protocol is established. Please see Kiss #19 for an idea for this one.

Sex Drive: Those who have a monthly cycling hormonal sequence have a *rhythmic* sex drive—not something most of us learn about. When this is understood, you'll know which kisses to focus on and when. Read the book, *4 Seasons in 4 Weeks*, for more information.

Final thoughts: The hope is that no matter how experienced your kissing is or how advanced your courting and foreplay skills are, you'll find a few new kisses in this book to try or some new thoughts to consider.

Whether you're here for the education or just the fun, ENJOY!

One

The First Kiss

Of course, our first kiss must be "The First Kiss."

Whether you're five or ninety-five, this is, perhaps, the sweetest and most enchanting of them all. Landing on either the lips or a cheek, giving a kiss is a brave action initiated by whoever dares to make a move when struck by Cupid. Trusting the feeling is mutual, the opportunity is a *now or never* situation, where one finds themself going for it.

Sometimes, "The First Kiss" is launched and also received unexpectedly. Other times it is anticipated.

Either make it magical.

To be clear, "The First Kiss" doesn't necessarily have to be your very *first* kiss. It's the very first kiss that was *meaningful*, a kiss

1

that was a turning point for you personally or for a budding relationship, or perhaps, your education. It's "The First Kiss" that stayed with you; a kiss that was special and still makes you smile (and melt) when you think about it; "The First Kiss" is a *marked point* in your life's journey; a kiss that changed you from there on out.

QUESTIONS

1. Do you have a memorable "First Kiss"?
2. When and where was it?
3. What are your thoughts about "The First Kiss?"

Two

The Plant

Is it possible to name the perfect kiss?

It all comes down to personal preference and opinion, of course, but the perfect kiss *does* have to meet specific subtle criteria:

- It has to be transformational, not routine, even when two people master it to the point of becoming their routine. Once it is taken for granted, it is no longer the perfect kiss.
- It has to cause both parties to experience momentary paralysis—the kind that causes the mind to forget *everything*—as if zapped by a slow and tantalizing stun gun.
- The perfect kiss is tender, bonding, and reassuring, creating a simple understanding and feeling of ONENESS.

I know such a kiss, and I call it: "The Plant."

This kiss is dazzling for so many reasons, even though the name isn't all that inspiring. First off, although simple in concept, it is rather tricky to get right, and you'll rarely see it done well. That's because it needs to be executed deliberately and mindfully with one's positive and total focus zeroed in on one's person-of-affection (poa), even if the poa is unaware that the kiss is coming and the person delivering it is in a hurry and has a lot on their mind. It's like watching a video that cuts to a slow-motion effect. This is a kiss that makes time stand still, even if for just a nanosecond. It's perfect because it is perfectly planted.

The Technique

"The Plant" is a soft but *confident* kiss that lands precisely right in every way—not too hard, not too light, not too sloppy or off-kilter. It lasts not too long nor too short. The lips are relaxed and slightly open—it's not an open-mouthed kiss. The bottom and top lips align even if they are different sizes. This is not a make-out session, just an affectionate meeting of the lips *with no tongue* that pauses just enough to enjoy it before it's gone.

"The Plant" is more manageable and intimate if the Lead cradles the jaw or neck with their hand to ensure the passion anchors itself well. Eyes close for just the perfect beat while the breath relaxes and slightly sighs. Before parting, both pairs of lips pull and melt together, then release the seal with a discreet sound. A look in the eyes, knowing smiles (and possibly a wink), follows.

It's pretty delicious.

The Plant

"The Plant" is the foundational, romantic kiss for several approaches that we'll explore a little later. It is the kiss that lingers on one's lips for a day and sometimes a lifetime. Done in the right place at the right time, it can be absolutely unforgettable.

Whether at home or in public, "The Plant" is the most enthralling kiss of all for saying hello and goodbye to one's partner. I witnessed one person greeting their sweetie with it, and I remember the first time I received it myself. Both took me by surprise, and both instances stopped me in my tracks.

WOW. I felt mine on my lips for weeks.

Warning: "The Plant" can be shared between casual intimates, but take caution: This kiss creates hard-to-shake feelings, and it's even harder to forget. This is a kiss that speaks the language of meaning. Better use of this one would be between committed couples or people who would like to take their relationship to the next level. When done with mindfulness, appreciation, and gratitude for the other, this kiss may serve as both aphrodisiac and good medicine for a long and close relationship.

QUESTIONS

1. What do you feel about "The Plant?"
2. Do you have a different kiss that you feel is the perfect kiss?
3. Do you have a special story about "The Plant?"

Three

The Lip-lock

W hile "The Plant" is delivered with lips relaxed and *slightly* open and with no tongue, "The Lip-lock" kiss is an *open-mouthed* "Plant" kiss. Tongues might be exchanged in the process (or not).

The Technique

As both parties dive in for a kiss, they *subtly* open their mouths before locking lips.

Here's the difference:

With "The Plant," the lips are positioned as if you're taking a sip of water from a glass. For the "Lip-lock," your mouth opens as if you're taking a bite of something from your fork. In other words, you're not opening your mouth enough to have someone take a look at your tonsils, but just enough to create a small or large "O," depending on the mouth you're kissing. With "The Plant," your lips need to be naturally relaxed and soft, and with "The Lip-lock," your lips open to create an "O" while also staying soft.

The best example I've seen of this, where you can actually see it happen, is in the movie *The Holiday*. Both Jude Law and Cameron Diaz take the same approach as the other and together nail "The Lip-lock."

Warning: If you, as the Lead approach all kisses with a "Lip-lock" style but the Receiver isn't expecting a kiss and has closed or relaxed lips, "The Lip-lock" might overwhelm and surround the Receiver's lips rather than hit the target. Keep your eyes open and on their lips to get it right.

Rule of thumb: If you're saying hello or goodbye to a *friend* (and not an intimate), make it "The Plant," (without lingering), not "The Lip-lock." Or instead, go for a cheek kiss (see Kiss #19). They are actually clearer and classier in the long run.

QUESTIONS

1. Have you ever experienced "The Lip-lock?"
2. Do you have a unique story about "The Lip-lock?"

Four

Parlez-vous français ?

"The French Kiss." It's everyone's rite-of-passage kiss.

Like "The Plant", "The French Kiss" (aka, "tongue-twisting) is a foundational kiss from which other kisses are born. We will visit many of them in the following chapters.

There are as many good ways to "French Kiss" as there are people, and there are many bad ways. Yet, good and bad "French Kissing" is a personal preference. Whatever the approach, "The French Kiss", *more than any other kiss*, is about matching the other person's vibration. It is the most *physically* intimate of kisses because the parties share breath, exchange saliva, body chemistry, and intertwine vulnerability.

This kiss is literally personal.

Parlez-vous français ?

The Technique

- This kiss can be approached as "The Lip-lock" with mouths opening as they come together and meet, *or* as "The Plant" where lips come together relaxed and *then* open.
- Begin slowly. Allow your tongue to touch and explore the other person's tongue and mouth.
- Find a breathing rhythm and keep everything soft, steady, and smooth. Relax into it.

Well done!

QUESTIONS

1. Do you remember your first "French Kiss?"
2. Is it a pleasant memory?
3. Do you have a special story or "French Kiss?"

Five

The Lip Liner

"T he Lip Liner" kiss is just as it sounds and adds a little interest to "The French Kiss."

I like this one, *and* a little goes a long way. Best not to overdo it. Consider this an accent piece for your "French Kiss" toolbox. Do it briefly and then move on. Repeat occasionally.

The Technique

I think "The Lip Liner" works best once "French Kissing" is up and fully functioning.

Somewhere in there, take the slightly-relaxed tip of your tongue and begin to outline the outside edge of the Receiver's lips. The tongue should not be overly wet. Go around the entire mouth at a focused pace—it's not a race, and you're not asleep either. Just be present and enjoy. Match your partner's vibe. The idea for this one is for it to simply be intriguing for both people—something a little different—an out-of-the-toolbox surprise.

Do this for one spin (or maybe two) around the mouth and call it good.

If you prefer, instead of going around the outer lip line, follow the center of the lips for one full circle. This one is pretty luscious. And then there is the inside edge of the lips to trace.

Uh-huh.

QUESTIONS

1. Have you ever done "The Lip Liner" on anyone or had it done to you?
2. What are your thoughts about "The Lip Liner?"
3. Do you have a luscious story about "The Lip Liner?"

Six

The Wrapper

"The Wrapper" is quite a nice kiss. In my opinion, it should be a staple in everyone's "French Kiss" toolbox. Once mastered, it's dreamy.

The Technique

Once things are going nicely with "French Kissing," wrap your *lips* around your partner's *tongue* and begin to suck and glide on it with an in and out motion. Do this only once or twice and then release unless more feels needed. Usually, less is better. The whole thing makes for a nice accent move.

Know that you have to time this one just right, kind of like jumping *into* a simple Double Dutch jump rope situation. It's best if you don't go *after* your partner's tongue. In other words, don't be diving into their mouth to lasso and wrangle it.

Instead, gently seize it and take charge of it when their tongue is your territory. Make this smooth, and then let go and do something else. Your partner will most likely reciprocate. When they do, you'll find out how surprisingly erotic it is.

Troubleshooting: If you're timid, you might not be able to grasp that slippery, moving target. So plan to go after it and lock onto it—no teeth. If you don't suction up, you won't suck easily. Start with handling just the tip of the tongue and if that goes well, go further. The bottom line is, just get in there and do it! In time, it will be totally organic, comfortable, and relaxing. Easy.

Weave this technique into your regular kissing session and perfect it as you go. :)

QUESTIONS:

1. Have you ever done "The Wrapper" on anyone or had it done to you?
2. Do you like "The Wrapper?"
3. Do you have a story about "The Wrapper?"

Seven

The Nipper

A nother excellent addition to your "French Kiss" toolbox is "The Nipper." As with any accent tool, use it sparingly.

The Technique

When "French Kissing," begin to alternate between sucking on and gently biting the *lower* lip. Do this two or three times, then go back to regular kissing. After that, approach another area of the lower lip and repeat. If it is easy enough to do with the *top* lip, try that here or there. Stimulating.

QUESTION

1. Do you have a special story about "The Nipper?"

Eight

The Pop

There are great kisses and good kisses, and then there are *not-great* kisses.

I know someone who disagrees with me (and you might too), but I find "The Pop" kiss quite annoying and even somewhat insulting. Yet, it's quite possibly the most performed kiss on the planet, or at least in the U.S. I feel sure that the person doing the popping has no idea what "not-a-kiss" this is, so please don't hear me blaming The Popper.

The Popper means well.

But here's the problem:

"The Pop" is less like a kiss and more like an accidental dive-bomb by a gigantic flying insect. "The Pop" is a *not-really* kiss that quickly bounces off your lips or cheek. It feels and looks obligatory. It's often done with pursed lips as if The Popper wants to get in and out as fast as possible—to give a kiss "for the record."

It's also known as a "peck."

Significant kisses are certainly not needed day in and day out. However, it is essential to give a mindful kiss or not bother. A kiss needs to be deliberate, something that the kisser wants to do.

The Technique

When saying hello or goodbye to your partner, purse your lips into a point and peck them on the lips or cheek. Then get in and out of the kiss as fast as you can. Not!

Holding the kiss for a second longer would allow the Receiver to enjoy the kiss and make "The Pop" an actual kiss— a sweet kiss. Better yet, replace this with "The Plant" kiss.

QUESTIONS

1. Do you like "The Pop?"
2. Do you have a kiss you particularly love or particularly can't stand?
3. Do you have an unusual story about "The Pop"?

Nine

The Vampire

"The Vampire" is flat-out, hell yes, sexy, leaving one's, er, victim, limp and a bit faint due to this kiss's ability to cause knee-buckling and heart-racing. But that's no problem because a big part and great thing about "The Vampire" is that your body is fully embraced, which means you won't fall to the floor while "The Vampire" is injecting body-numbing magic through your veins while stealing your ability to think. In other words, the embrace is part of the kiss.

Without the embrace, it wouldn't be "The Vampire."

The Technique

This kiss is done in a slow one, two, three-beat without stopping. Facing each other:

1. The Lead puts one arm around the Receiver's waist, placing their hand on the small of the back, pulling the Receiver into them, nice and snug.
2. Simultaneously, the Lead's other hand moves along the Receiver's jaw and back of the neck (the thumb is in front of the ear and the rest of the hand is behind) to guide and bring the targeted area (neck) toward the Lead's mouth while allowing the Receiver's head to fall back a bit.
3. The Lead sloooowly dives into the opened-up side of the neck.

Now, from here...the Lead has many choices:

Option 1: The lips barely touch the neck. Instead, the nose takes the lead, slowly exploring the scent of the Receiver's neck, inhaling and exhaling as seen fit and in response to the Receiver's breathing. Avoid tickling because it will keep the Receiver from relaxing into the action.

Option 2: The lips place themselves onto the Receiver's neck, but lightly, allowing the lips to do the feeling. This action is best done as a secret rendezvous done in a public place where the couple must appear to only be hugging. The Lead then begins enjoying said neck in slow, "barely there" kisses while the Receiver must remain composed. TORTURE! Not being able to respond when breathing becomes heavy (which it surely will) causes the Receiver to become heated *faster*. Which is what makes this approach absolutely DIVINE and wicked.

Option 3: Same as Option Two, it is done in private this time. The lips make a solid but soft, smooth landing and get to pleasurable work. This one is spine-and-all-places tingling, creating a loin rumble so surprising that it sends the blood rushing and spreading like hot lava throughout the Receiver's inner volcano.

Option 4: The mouth approaches WIDE-open and begins to suck on the neck while moving the tongue around in a slow, smooth, circular motion. The trick here is that the teeth must be out of the way so that this is an intoxicating experience. If you've never had this kiss done to you, have your sweetie (or even a friend) make this happen! The Lead should not suck so hard that a hickey results. That's too hard for this hypnotizing encounter.

Option 5: Same as #4, except a bit of gentle biting would be added to the mix.

Option 6: Take the tip of your tongue and do one *very long* and not-too-wet lick from your victim's sternum (top of chest) or sternal notch (space below the throat) up to the tip of their chin. Don't overdo it. Once is plenty for a breathtaking effect.

Sounds: As if all of that isn't enough, all "The Vampire" options can (and should) be supercharged with sounds of pleasure without getting weird about it.

If you are the Lead, never underestimate the importance of letting your partner know how much you love what you are tasting or smelling (no matter where it is on the body). *Insatiable* is even better and a compliment, as long as you're not overdoing it or not picking up on the Receiver's cues. Just get into it and enjoy the neck with all of your heightened senses. Allow yourself to be *primal*, letting your partner know that there is no other place you'd rather be.

If you are the Receiver, never underestimate the importance of letting your partner know that what is being done to you is pleasurable. No "faking it." Allow yourself to be 100% present, and your sounds will authentically express themselves. Allow yourself to let go and thoroughly enjoy.

BONUS VAMPIRE KISS! "The Ravenous"

Technique:

While "The Vampire" kiss is a sophisticated and composed approach to hypnotize the Receiver, "The Ravenous" *must have* the Receiver NOW!

Begin this kiss with the same moves as above. However, instead of putting lips to neck, go for the *mouth* with a hungry "Lip-lock." Go back and forth between the mouth and the neck. Maybe add a lick from neck to chin. Yep.

QUESTIONS

1. Has anyone done "The Vampire" on you?
2. Do you have an extraordinary story about "The Vampire?"
3. What about "The Ravenous?"

Ten

The Back-of-the-Neck Vampire

I n the same way that "The Vampire Kiss" is a win-win exchange of euphoria between the Lead and the Receiver, "The Back-of-the-Neck Vampire" is just as disarming and breathtaking (if not more), allowing even the busiest Receiver to take a moment from their hectic schedule to surrender fully while the Lead feeds.

Don't forget that vampires excel at putting their victims into a trance. In this case, it is a fine thing indeed. The (side) back of one's neck is the most accessible place to put the Receiver under one's spell without difficulty.

My question is, why isn't this kiss utilized often? It is seriously, out of this world. The relaxed, sensuous approach is what makes this kiss sophisticated, erotic, and exquisite—all at the same time.

Mostly what makes the "Back" version different from the "Front" version is *control by the Receiver.* When The Receiver is facing their partner, one has complete control of their arms and can adjust body positions should it be needed. But when the Lead is behind the Receiver, it's more difficult for the Receiver to take charge of anything. This is what makes this kiss dangerously erotic.

The Receiver is both captive and *captivated* in this one.

The Technique

Standing, the Lead snuggles up behind their *poa and places one hand up high along the Receiver's shoulder. The other hand goes to the same side and then sweeps the hair to the opposite side if needed, clearing room and making space for the Lead's desire. That same hand anchors itself on that opposite side and pulls the neck closer and into position.

The Lead dives in and begins to *slowly* explore the cleared area with a few deliciously planted kisses (See "The Plant" kiss), or a few sucks and nibbles.

There are many fantastic ways to enhance this one:

1. Massage the Receiver's shoulders first until relaxed,
2. then naturally move into "The Back-of-the-Neck Vampire."
3. Lightly stroke the Receiver's shoulders before or while you're doing this kiss.

Just pay attention to how your poa responds to all of them. Get creative! Keep it slow and steady.

"The Back-of-the-Neck" Vampire is incredibly easy to do and can be done casually in any setting or voraciously in private. It's up to you.

QUESTIONS

1. Have you ever actually had anyone do "The Back-of-the-Neck Vampire" on you?
2. What are your thoughts about "The Back-of-the-Neck Vampire?"
3. Do you have a tantalizing story about "The Back-of-the-Neck Vampire?"

*person of affection

Eleven

The Vampirate

⚜

"The Vampirate" takes a very different turn and differentiates itself from the previous Vampire kisses. It includes risk and the love of pirates.

The following happened to me personally, so I feel I'm an expert on what to do and what not to do when wearing a pirate hat and donning razor-sharp *vampire teeth*. I recommend the cross-costuming, but please heed my warnings: no guarantees, but the night could get very sexy and possibly dangerous depending on the party atmosphere.

While pirates and vampires tend to be society's dark faves any time of the year, it was, in fact, Halloween. What better time to bring otherworldly swashbucklers and bloodsuckers through the veils simultaneously?

However, my thought process didn't start out this way. While certainly, both pirates and vampires are my secret loves, as a writer, one day, I simply saw how the two words fit together and wondered why it wasn't a thing. Or perhaps it *is* a thing in some cult-classic low-budget horror movie or YA fantasy novel, but I hadn't heard the term before. I'm probably just not in the know.

Anyhow, this solved that particular year's dilemma of what to be for Halloween. Naturally, I'd go as a "Vampirate." As in, *vampire pirate*.

It ended up being a super fun night (and somewhat wild) with my friends. We went to a large, spirited event and eventually slipped away to a small party. From the beginning, I ended up discovering something I hadn't at all expected: that humans find sharp canines to be an arousing, sexy feature. Who knew? Everywhere I went, gender or no gender party-goers wanted to experience my teeth on their necks—or become a vampire themselves by diving into *my* neck or my mouth-with-teeth for a quick make-out moment. Wow! I rolled with it, because after all, how often does that happen?

I began to enjoy the power of my fangs. I loved the fact that one person, about half my age, kept begging me to sink my teeth into their neck. I made a few rounds of the venue before I gave in. I was certainly game for it, but I was acutely aware that I could do severe damage or worse—as I said, the teeth were super sharp, and I felt they would definitely puncture if I wasn't careful. But this person was a willing volunteer, so I decided to give it a go.

The Technique

I figured out that the best technique was to slowly *tap* the sharpness into their neck a few times, then finish the job by sealing my lips around the area so that I could do a quick "French Kiss" and suck motion, then release. Of course, we had to try that out a few times to make sure we got it right—you know, practice makes perfect. And then we tried it a few more times for good measure. That neck smelled really, really (did I say really?) *appetizing*. I knew right then and there that my true inner vampire had completely taken over. I had crossed into the dark side.

But as long as I applied my teeth responsibly and didn't linger too long, I could do no wrong with this new superpower, and I liked it! I honestly hadn't had that much fun, maybe ever.

Once home, I removed the vampire teeth, brushed my *real* teeth, and went to bed. But then, I woke up in the morning. From my lips to the inside of my cheeks to the back of my throat, my mouth was fully swollen! The sharp edges of my canines had completely torn everything up while I was doing my best "Vampirate" work throughout the night. It took many days for it to heal.

So, the thing I learned?

File your vampire teeth down to the place where they still look scary but aren't actually sharp enough to do damage. The sensation for others will still be chilling, but your mouth won't have to suffer the consequences.

The Teeth: First off, you have to find the real deal. I imagine you can get the teeth at a big box Halloween store but, I'm not sure. I got mine at a smaller costumery. At the time, they were about $23 (U.S.).

Yes, they are a commitment.

The teeth take some prep, so don't wait until the last minute when things are hectic on Halloween night before going out. Read the instructions early on and plan your timing.

Party Safety

1. No matter your age, be observant and aware.
2. Go with at least one friend and leave with that friend or friends. A group is best.
3. Watch out for and keep track of one another.
4. Know where you are—the location of the party or venue.
5. Party responsibly in all ways. The worst that you want to wake up with is a swollen mouth from your vampire teeth.

QUESTIONS

1. Have you ever been a "Vampirate?"
2. What are your thoughts about "The Vampirate?"
3. Do you have a fun story about wearing vampire teeth?

Twelve

The Hickey

Let's face it. "The Hickey" is a timeless teenage badge of making-out success!

Basically, it's a bruise on the neck. A hickey needs to go where it can be seen from the front or side; otherwise, hair or a collar might cover it up. *That* would ruin everything since "The Hickey" serves as a declaration to ALL that you are indeed "getting some" or sexually active in some way in case anyone was curious or doubted your abilities to attract a mate.

It sort of makes my neck hurt to think about it, as the ones I ended up with weren't very comfortable in the receiving of them. Still, sometimes the pain is worth it. With a teen (or even an adult), cool always outweighs not-cool. And there's nothing wrong with carrying a souvenir and a reminder of your time together.

The Technique

I want to say that I believe this goes faster and easier for people with well-endowed lips than people with thin lips because it's *a must* to get good suction between the perimeter of the lips and your *poa's skin. But if your lips are thin, no worries. Just latch onto a portion of the neck where your lips fit more easily.

Next, suck and enjoy the taste of your poa and keep your teeth out of the way. You actually have to enjoy the neck enough to *slightly* break the capillaries but not so hard that you're hurting your love interest. There's a balance in there. Go for a little bit, then stop and probably repeat. It's sort of a trial and error thing. At first, it will most likely be red, so be careful to not overdo it, or the morning light will bring something much darker than intended and will take much longer to get rid of. You and your poa want to look cool, not desperate. Either way, the hickey and both of your reputations will be solid no matter how it turns out.

QUESTIONS

1. Have you ever had a hickey or given one?
2. What are your thoughts about "The Hickey?"
3. Do you have a story about "The Hickey?"

*person-of-affection

Thirteen

The Purse

~~~∽◦❦◦∼~~~

P ursed lips happen when the muscles of the lips are tightened into a "bunch" which feels rigid to the Receiver. The good news? "The Purse" kiss is an easy fix. Pursed lips can happen with thin or full lips, but generally aren't noticed *quite* as much with full lips because no matter what is going on with the rigid muscles, there is still a pillowy landing for the Receiver. Thin lips, not so much. The exception to this would be chapped lips. That's not a great experience with either type of lips. See more on this in the intro chapter on kissing etiquette.

There are a couple of reasons why you might purse your lips:

1. It's protective. You don't want someone kissing you or don't want your "hello" kiss to be mistaken as an intimate intention.

2. You're not aware you're doing it, since things feel fine from your end of the kiss

The Fix

1. Get over your possible worry about it and ask your partner or a trusted friend to kiss and evaluate a "hello or goodbye" type of kiss. This is "The Plant" kiss without holding it for the extra beat or as sensually. Definitely no tongue with this test. Also avoid doing "The Pop."
2. If the evaluation comes back as a "Yes, you're pursing your lips," then evaluate which mouth muscles you're using.
3. Using the front and center muscles will cause pursing.
4. Try switching to the back corner muscles of you mouth (gently—not too tightly!), which automatically relaxes the front center muscles. This way, you'll still have control of the kiss, but it will feel soft to the Receiver. This is a mouth exercise that you can do on your own to get the hang of it.
5. When kissing intimately, relax those back muscles more, which will allow your mouth to open a bit or a lot, in order to get into the kiss.
6. Take your practiced mouth muscles back to your kissing evaluator for another test drive.

Without you realizing it, the way you kiss can change over time, due to non-use or being in a relationship where the intimacy style simply changed the way you now kiss. Don't be afraid to reevaluate so that you can get back to great, soft kissing!

Fourteen

The Peppermint

"The Peppermint" is the first of a few sensory journeys in this series, and it's pretty simple.

The Technique

After kissing for a bit, stop and add a drop or two of ingestible peppermint essential oil onto your tongue. Breath drops or spray will also work. Whatever you use needs to be much stronger than peppermint gum. It needs to feel somewhat icy.

Resume kissing. :)

To supercharge the peppermint, take a few sips of ice water! Be careful not to burn your mouth because of the intensity of the peppermint. Perhaps do a test run at another time when not kissing to get a feel for what you can handle.

The Peppermint

The Peppermint is particularly romantic when kissing outside in the snow and refreshing on the hottest day of summer. Sense-sational.

By the way, this technique is "whoa!" exciting when the mouth is applied to other, um, areas of the body. Please check in with your partner first —no exceptions on this point because private parts are ultra-sensitive to peppermint (or anything like it) and can burn if overdone. A tiny bit goes a long way. Start slowly. If it's a go, it can be a very stimulating experience indeed.

Alternative Approach: **"The Ice"**

Ditch the peppermint idea and just go for ice!.

1. The Lead (but not the Receiver) puts ice cubes in their mouth until the tongue, lips, and interior of the cheeks are icy cold.
2. The Lead leans in, and "French Kisses" the Receiver.
3. Feeling cooled off yet?
4. If not, just take the ice cubes and rub them all over each other!

QUESTIONS

1. Have you ever done "The Peppermint" on anyone or had it done to you?
2. What are your thoughts about "The Peppermint?"
3. Do you have a stimulating story about "The Peppermint?"

Fifteen

The Hot

L ike "The Peppermint" kiss, "The Hot" is one of the "sense-sational" kisses. The sense-sational kisses are all about the temperature or other effect on the Receiver, rather than the kissing technique itself.

The Technique

1. The Lead (but not the Receiver) takes a few sips of a hot beverage. I suggest tea over all other hot beverage choices because it tends to be the cleanest and most neutral, breath-wise.
2. Make sure the mouth and tongue are well heated, and then slowly "French Kiss" your *poa. Then take another sip and repeat.

Unlike "The Peppermint" kiss, "The Hot" is not stimulating.

However, a soft hot kiss can be a pleasant surprise that activates a melting of your honey's stressed body and mind. I liken the sensation to having an extra-warm towel applied to your face during a spa treatment or trip to the barber. Perhaps it's a warm blanket placed over you in a cold room. Either way, it's usually the perfect medicine that allows one to deepen into relaxation.

Dreamy.

Extra-curricular: If your mouth decides to explore *other parts of the Receiver's terrain* because said Receiver is indicating approval and a desire for more, continue to take sips of your hot beverage along the way. Obviously, don't burn your tongue or their body parts.

"The Hot" kiss makes for a cozy sensory journey during bone-chilling times. Take your thermos with you when you venture out.

BONUS KISS! "The Hot and Icy."

The Set-Up: Get two mugs. Put hot tea in one and ice water in the other.

The Technique

1. The Lead takes a few sips of the hot tea to get the mouth toasty warm and proceeds to "French Kiss" the Receiver.
2. The Lead then takes a few sips of the ice water until the tongue, lips, and interior of the cheeks are icy cold. The Lead then "French Kisses" the Receiver again.

3. One should take their time until the temperatures of the beverages lose their effect.
4. Continue to alternate between the two sensations.
5. Once complete, then…replenish your mugs and SWITCH ROLES.

QUESTIONS

1. Have you ever tried "The Hot" or "The Hot and Icy?"
2. What are your thoughts about these kisses?
3. Do you have any stories about them to share?

*person of affection

Sixteen

The Bones

This kiss is surprisingly sweet and erotic. "The Bones" is a good one to do independently or during downtime when making love.

The Technique

With bodies warm and a good connection made:

1. Begin to plant slow, methodical kisses on your *poa's facial bones: cheeks, eyes, jaw.
2. Then move down a bit further to the clavicle and shoulder.
3. Then back up to the jaw again or further down to explore the body.
4. Be sure to actually kiss the bones and hold your lips there for a beat as you go. The nerves between bone and skin deliver a lovely, soothing sensation to your partner.

Like some other kisses, a little goes a long way, so perhaps sweep the face and neck area one time and call it good. Overdoing it could be annoying—but understated can be comforting and caring. And it is a relaxing kiss for the Lead to deliver.

QUESTIONS

1. Have you ever done "The Bones" on anyone or had it done to you?
2. What are your thoughts about "The Bones?"
3. Do you have a special story** about "The Bones?"

*person of affection

Seventeen

The Lady and the Tramp

"The Lady and the Tramp" kiss involves food.

This kiss became famous in 1955 when the animated Disney movie *Lady and the Tramp* opened in theaters. It has remained one of the most famous dinner scenes in Hollywood history, not to mention one of the most romantically well done. There is nothing not to love about this scene.

The movie is based on a cocker spaniel named Lady who, for various reasons, finds herself out on the frightening streets—lost from her well-to-do-home. She is befriended by the street-wise Tramp, a mutt who knows his way around and the best places to get scraps. He takes Lady to the back door of an Italian restaurant where the owner, Tony, sees that Tramp (who Tony calls "Butch") has a lady-friend and treats them to a plate of spaghetti and meatballs. Tony and his chef, Joe, add to the evening by serenading the two canines to the gorgeous ballad, *Belle Notte*. While the setting works its magic, Lady and Tramp unknowingly begin eating the opposite ends of one spaghetti noodle until they come together in a kiss. I feel sure that's how the word "canoodling" got started.

I actually saw this kiss being done just after deciding to write about it and couldn't believe my eyes. When having lunch at a restaurant one day, a young couple and their two children were sitting in my view. When their food arrived, the couple was still getting their kids settled. The woman picked up what I think was a long slice of zucchini and put one end in her mouth. Motioning to her man, he readily obliged and attached his mouth to the other end, where they came together in a quick kiss. It was a lovely gesture in the middle of kid chaos and obviously something they do quite often to stay intimately connected.

And that's how it's done. Keep your love alive with one vegetable or noodle at a time.

Suggestion: Track this scene down online.

QUESTIONS

1. Have you ever tried "The Lady and the Tramp?"
2. Do you have any sweet stories about "The Lady and the Tramp?

Eighteen

The Global

Technically a greeting more than a kiss, "The Global" is what I'm calling the classic "cheek-to-cheek" hello and goodbye. To me, it still qualifies. I really love this acknowledgment because it seems to combine just the right elements for starting things out well.

This greeting is done all over Europe and parts of Russia, Africa, and other various countries, yet the general idea doesn't seem to have an "umbrella" name. The French call it *la bise (kiss)*, and the Italians call it *il bacetto* (the kiss) or *il saluto* (the greeting), for instance. Culturally, regionally, and depending on how well you know the person, this greeting varies a LOT. In many places, this "cheek-to-cheek" kiss is done between men and women and women to women, with men shaking hands. However, again, it depends on the location. So for our *50 kisses* and traveling know-how, I will keep it simple and go for the basic idea.

41

The Technique

Let's choose to go for the left side first, the Receiver's right. All instructions apply to both people at the same time.

1. Make eye contact.
2. Step forward but not too close.
3. Anchor your hand on the Receiver's right shoulder or arm.
4. Go for the left side by extending your right cheek.
5. Touch cheeks only, and kiss the air with the kiss sound.
6. Move to the other cheek and repeat. This greeting has a nicely balanced pace when facing your person and moving from the left to the right and then done.

Suggestion: When traveling, first watch how the locals do it before getting tangled up by beginning on the wrong side or not kissing enough times. Shake hands instead if that's what they do.

QUESTIONS

1. Have you ever tried "The Global?"
2. What are your thoughts about "The Global?"
3. Do you have a beautiful story about "The Global?"

Nineteen

The Nice-to-See-You

⚬⚬⚬

"The Nice-to-See-You" kiss is the perfect *greeting* for family, good friends, and friendly acquaintances, at least in the United States and perhaps other places that don't do a version of "The Global." This kiss would also fall under "The Global" umbrella.

When greeting your friends, if kissing on the lips is what you do and it works for you and them, then, by all means, proceed! But if you find this to be awkward at times, there is a reason for it.

Namely…kissing on the lips is *intimate*. Deeply intimate.

We've gotten pretty casual about kissing on the lips but it's never *not* been intimate. We just don't talk about it. But because it *is*, the whole thing can get tricky. The problem with kissing hello or goodbye on the lips is that it happens quickly and can sometimes go wonky *or perfectly* and both can have us pondering it too long afterward. Did we just miss each other's mouths? Did that person intend to make it that juicy? Did I purse up and give a "Pop" because I was afraid I'd do or allow a "Plant" and give the wrong impression? Or "WOW, that was nice." And then there are other problems such as jealousy from partners or not wanting to kiss the person who is kissing you hello.

The ideal hello/goodbye kiss on the lips would be a "Plant" without a beat, but the problem is, if it lands perfectly, it will still linger on the lips a little too long. This can set into motion thinking that is probably better left not set into motion. Kissing on the lips is fun with friends you know well, share affection with, totally trust, and have a mutual understanding that this is all it is and that's that.

For everyone else, "The Nice to See You" kiss is my solution. It can be done formally or warmly.

The Technique

"The Nice-to-See-You" is a kiss on the cheek done by both people when saying hello or goodbye. It's like "The Global" except that it is *one* kiss, as opposed to two or more that go from side to side, and the kiss actually lands on the cheek, rather than in the air.

This kiss begins with what you decide to do with your hands.

1. Handshake - Shake with your right hand and continue to lean in to kiss each other's right cheek at the same time.
2. Shoulder: Put one or both hands on the Receiver's shoulders or arms and then lean into the left to kiss each other's right cheek.
3. Hug, and both of you kiss each other's right cheek.
4. Heart-to-heart hug: Hug to the right side (hugging hearts) and kiss each other's left cheek.

If at work, or when meeting people for the first time, follow the lead of those around you, but generally a handshake will be the appropriate action. Be sure to look them in the eye as you do so.

QUESTIONS

1. What is your preferred way to greet friends and family?
2. Do you have any stories of kisses being awkward?
3. What do you think of "The Nice to See You" kiss?

Twenty

The Hollywood

"The Hollywood" is the same kiss as "The Global", only opposite in pretty much every way.

OK, actually, "The Hollywood" is a "Global-*wanna-be*" with drama and flair.

That's why it's called "The Hollywood!"

You'll see this kiss when your most flamboyant friend walks into the party fashionably late with their coat on and arms full of incredible goods: a plate of the most divine, expensive cheese *ever*, a gift for the hostess, and of course, a bottle of George Clooney's tequila. Lots of smiles and hellos.

A few drinks may have already been consumed.

The Technique

Going for the left side first (the Receiver's right), act like you're going to touch or kiss cheeks, but don't. The cheeks don't actually touch. It's an air thing in every way. Not only are you simply holding too much stuff to anchor a hand on someone's shoulder, but why would you risk getting germs, especially if you aren't sure you like the person all that much? So best not to get too close. Instead, kiss the wind with a loud "MUAAAH" and repeat quickly on the other side.

Despite its possible insincerity, it actually *is* a FABULOUS way to enter a room and get the party rolling. So there's nothing not to love about that.

QUESTIONS

1. Have you ever tried "The Hollywood?"
2. What are your thoughts about "The Hollywood?"
3. Do you have an outlandish story about "The Hollywood?"

Twenty-One

The Giver and the Receiver

I've been using the term "The Receiver" to indicate the person being kissed. This is still the case, but *this time* it is also part of the description and point of the kiss itself.

Although "The Giver and the Receiver" is a *fun* kiss for any two people, it is primarily a kiss for *self-improvement* between committed couples. Self-improvement leads to relationship-improving.

Doesn't kissing sound like the best kind of therapy?

The Point: "The Giver and the Receiver" is an intentional experiment between two people, where both get an opportunity to feel the lips of the other. One is experiencing full giving without receiving anything in return and the other is receiving without feeling the need to give anything in return.

For the Lead, this kiss is actually an exercise in *giving* for the pure joy of it and because the Lead actually wants the Receiver to receive a gift. It's an exercise in giving without manipulating or angling for acknowledgment, approval, or attention. It is an exercise in communicating rather than buying (or giving) one's way out of connecting heart-to-heart. Can the Lead honestly give without expectation?

For the Receiver, it is an exercise in releasing control to receive or take without feeling guilty or perhaps, needing to reciprocate to keep score or out of obligation, or worse, feeling they now *owe* the other person and fear of retribution down the road if they don't pay up in some way. It's an exercise to see if the Receiver can fully receive just because they deserve to receive. Can the receiver honestly receive without stress?

It's an exercise in trust between two people and in simply being present. But ultimately, it's an opportunity for each person to self-evaluate their needs, neediness, expectations, obligations, manipulative practices, fears, and boundaries.

This all comes in handy when it is time to give and receive physical gifts or any sweet offer.

The Technique

The goal would be to give without expectation and to receive without stress. Gratitude and appreciation for the other are a must for the long run. Both must enter this kissing exercise with an open and loving heart to observe their internal reactions and thoughts.

1. Position-wise, both the Receiver and the Lead must be comfortable.
2. The Receiver could choose to be sitting in a chair, on a stool, on the floor, or even lying down.
3. The Lead needs to be able to lean in for a kiss comfortably.
4. Try this kiss with a blindfold or no blindfold to feel more present and in the moment. Each must be able to trust that they are in a safe environment.
5. As the Lead goes in for the kiss, the Receiver (on purpose and in a disciplined way) does nothing to greet this kiss other than keep said lips soft, still, and natural. This action (or inaction) should not be mistaken for dissing the Lead.
6. The Lead then delivers a kiss that doesn't require the Receiver to interact. For instance, "The French Kiss" would be OUT, but "The Plant" or "The Bones" would definitely be IN and good ones to start with. Check the *50 Kisses* list. You'll notice there are many that qualify. A hug could also be used. "The Vampire" kisses are good ones, but those are more advanced and probably best left until you've done a more basic version first.
7. Feel free to do one or more kisses. If you go for two or three kisses, give time in between so that the Receiver may notice their internal responses. A journal may be used.
8. Once the exercise is complete, thank each other. Then REVERSE ROLES and REPEAT. :)

PLEASE NOTE: This kissing technique can also be used as a sexier and more deeply intimate full-bodied activity if desired. Use your imagination…

QUESTIONS and NOTES

1. What kind of "Giver" are you?
2. What sort of "Receiver?"
3. How did you feel when you played each role?
4. Did you like this exercise?
5. What would you like to try next time?
6. What kind of feelings came up for you in each role about yourself?
7. What came up for you about your partner?

Notes:

Twenty-Two

The Tug

I don't really know how many people are into this one, but I don't think it is that common. I've only had one *poa actually do this, and I soon realized it was part of his regular kissing routine. I call it "The Tug." I'm still not sure whether I liked it or not. But I did like *him*. He was fun.

"The Tug" was definitely surprising and intriguing, yet it was also distracting and annoying. I think it was the fact that it seemed a bit dramatic for saying hello or goodbye. Perhaps it would be a good move and make a better statement during a moment of super-heightened passion, used sparingly even then.

This guy's go-to was *hair* tugging—the type that could be done on short or long hair.

The HAIR TUG Technique

He'd start with a full-bodied embrace and kiss. But instead of putting one hand behind my neck, he'd go higher and slide his fingers through my hair along my scalp to hold my head and then just grab a chunk and tug. And then he'd tug some more.

Sometimes it was more like a caveman thing as he asserted his masculine control or whatever. Other times it was repeated rhythmically in how a satisfied cat gets into purring and kneading with its claws.

I'll just leave you with all of that to consider.

SAFETY: I also saw The Tug as a potential red flag. It was a slight tug at first, but how rough would it or *he* get down the road? As time went on, it seemed clear there was nothing to worry about with this sweet guy. But I still think it is something to pay attention to. Hair grabbing is often used to control the victim in assaults.

When *The Tug* is a total NO-NO: If you don't know if the Receiver (of any gender or ethnicity) has hair extensions or anything of the kind in their hair, you don't want to tug on it until you know, or else you could be in for a rude awakening with a kick to the privates, a slap in the face, or a ferocious talking to.

Never assume. "The Tug" is a bold move all on its own. You don't need to add to the risk.

BONUS TUG! Here, your significant other needs to have a *long beard.*

The BEARD TUG Technique

When walking up to say hello, gently but firmly gather and grab the beard and pull your sweetheart's mouth to yours. *Plant* your best kiss.

Do that in front of his friends. He'll thank you later.

Final thoughts regarding both Tug kisses: When used *sparingly* and with a trusted partner, The Tug can be an erotic and effective way to bring heated passion to the mix. I say, add it here and there.

QUESTIONS

1. Have you ever tried "The Tug"—hair or beard?
2. What are your thoughts about "The Tug?"
3. Do you have a special story about "The Tug?"

*person of affection

Twenty-Three

The Muzzle Nuzzle

❧❧❧

T his used to be called "The Eskimo Kiss," but as could be expected, The Eskimo Kiss isn't really an Eskimo *kiss*. Nor is *Eskimo* an accepted term for many/most of the Northern Indigenous peoples. Some still use it; however, much of the word-origin research shows the name has a derogatory and racist history beginning with European colonizers (surprise, surprise!), so it's best not to use it. Although Arctic people from Greenland, Canada, and Alaska have their own names and ways, *Inuit* is the accepted general term, simply meaning "people." The singular is *Inuk*, which means "person."

Now that we've got that clear let's talk about the kiss. Which is not a kiss.

Nor is it a nose-to-nose interaction. For the most part, the Inuit kiss is an affectionate *nuzzle* between family and friends called a *Kunik*. And depending on where you're from, it varies on how it's done and who it is between. In some places, it is only done by parents and children and in others, between partners, for instance.

According to Inuit TicTokers, @shinanova, and her mother, @kayuulanova, a Kunik is done "with emotion." The face, especially the cheeks, has many scent glands, and "The Kunik" is done by rubbing one's nose into the cheek of their loved one and sniffing to reacquaint oneself with this person's smell. The more you want to show affection, the harder you rub your nose into their cheek and sniff! This mother and daughter demonstrate and laugh after doing it. So that's "The Kunik."

And since the Eskimo Kiss is not an appropriate name and not a kiss that the Inuit do anyway, it would appear that **the original nose-to-nose kiss is nameless and up for grabs!** So why not claim it? It is flat-out adorable.

I'd like to call it "The Muzzle Nuzzle" (aka the nose-to-nose).

The Technique

1. Bring the tips of two participating noses together and rub them back and forth.

And there you have it. "The Muzzle Nuzzle." Cute.

Twenty-Four

The E-Zone

‿⟨᷼᷼⟩‿

"The E-Zone" is not a kiss but rather an area to *be* kissed, a secret spot to be discovered and worshiped.

Flirting, light touch, massage, kissing, and focusing on your *poa's erogenous zones (E-Zones) are necessary solo acts to keep affection alive and *crucial* if you want things to proceed further. While we know that our individual private parts are their own ecosystems of pleasure points, they are not the first to be touched unless you want a lackluster result. By knowing (or discovering) your partner's "E-Zones" and giving them your full attention first, you'll show your poa that there's no place you'd rather be. Which is a turn-on all on its own. It's the difference between being a good and not-so-good lover.

The skin itself contains an entire network of nerve endings, touch receptors, and messengers that, when stimulated, can create pleasurable responses that stand well on their own or lead to better sex than would be had without this touch. Depending on the person, the right attention to the right place at the right time can be better than sex itself simply by producing a purely pleasurable, full-body experience. Yep, one breathtaking "E-Zone" touch or set of kisses can do that.

"E-Zones" are far too overlooked. Let's give them a little more love!

So, where are these "E-Zones?" Erogenous zones are as individual as the individual. But, going from top to bottom, common spots include the scalp, temples, ears, *any part* of the neck, clavicle, shoulders, between the upper shoulder blades (my fave), any part of the back, inside of elbows, wrists, palms, fingers, ribs, hip bones, lower back, top or bottom of the butt, inner thighs, backs of knees, ankles, feet, and toes. Sometimes just touching or taking one's hand and tracing around the lines can be a very erotic gesture.

The Technique

If you know where one of your honey's "E-Zones" are, then lightly touch, kiss, lick, suck or massage it with a slow, measured rhythm. If you don't know where one is, ask them and/or experiment with a few of the locations I pointed out. Go slow enough to detect your poa's response. Do they want more of it or less by their breathing or relaxation?

One way to begin is to take your partner's hand, place your thumb into the center, and massage circles into it. Perhaps move up your poa's arm—applying this same pressure as you "step" along (see "The Gomez 2") or kiss their wrist. Continue with this massage or kiss technique in the neck area until your partner seems relaxed, and then explore the back and shoulder regions. There is no destination and no hurry, so there need not be expectations of the outcome. The idea is to give your poa pleasure and notice areas that respond more than others. If you discover one, do not forget it! This "E-Zone" can more easily flip your partner's switch from off to on—and often, immediately (as long as all is well with your relationship).

As I noted in the Introduction, even the simple act of holding hands is potent, sweet, and fun and provides feelings of security. So get into the habit of *occasionally* touching or kissing your partner's accessible "E-Zones" when out and about. For example, kiss your poa's shoulder or lightly scratch their back when standing in line someplace. It will make your everyday outings feel like a fun date that never ends and will supercharge your relationship into one of positivity, cooperation, and happiness.

Practice "The E-Zone" to keep your love life healthy. It's a titillating balm.

QUESTIONS

   1. Are "The E-Zones" something you pay attention to?
   2. Where are your "E-Zones?"

*person of affection

Twenty-Five

The Dart

S o…"The Dart." I don't like it. I understand, of course, that kissing is a personal preference thing, but I don't care for it in my mouth or in my ears. It's distracting and irritating. However, depending on the delivery, other body parts are probably a yes.

The Technique

"The Dart" is precisely that. When starting a "French Kiss," someone's tongue takes on a rapid-fire in-and-out darting motion with a pointy, rigid tongue. If it is long enough, it might push toward the back of the throat. The person doing it usually has no idea that this is way too much tongue being shoved into the other's domain, yet it's simply hard for the Receiver to relax and breathe together with this bull in a china shop.

And the *ear* "Dart" is awful. Forget that move unless you know your sweetheart likes it.

The Solution: If "The Dart" isn't your thing either, then show this book to your *poa and suggest trying out a kiss a day for 50 days. Then, perhaps "The Dart" will cease or diminish on its own. Or…suggest having "The Dart" done elsewhere to see if you like it there. If so, ask for more there and less in your mouth (or ears).

QUESTIONS

1. Have you ever given or received "The Dart?"
2. What are your thoughts about "The Dart?"
3. Do you have a special story about "The Dart?"

*person of affection

Twenty-Six

The Tongue-in-Cheek

"The Tongue-in-Cheek" is a cute, silly kiss to do on friends or little kids. But, then again, if you use your imagination, you might be able to turn it into something quite sensuous for your sweetie...

The Technique

1. Place your tongue against the inside of your cheek and push it out a bit.
2. Next, touch that cheek against someone's cheek and move your tongue around the inside of your cheek. You can practice it against your hand.
3. To the Receiver, the sensation feels fun, odd, and intriguing.

They'll laugh (or at least smile), and you probably will too.

62

Twenty-Seven

The Gomez 1

When growing up, Gomez and Morticia Addams left the biggest impression on me when it came to love, romance, and kinky sex.

Everything turned these two on.

And I'm pretty sure Gomez ruined me for life regarding how I want to be kissed. And adored. And worshiped. It's even probable that Gomez is responsible for most of my *50 Kisses* ideas. He does so many of them, so well (maybe even perfectly!), especially "The E-Zone."

These two teach us how *real* foreplay works, and it's done with the largest sex organ in the body: *the brain*. From there, physical instincts and practiced skills organically follow.

Because of this, I'm going to break down the Addams couple into three *50 Kisses* segments because each deserves to be highlighted. I'm calling them "The Gomez" 1, 2, and 3 because Gomez is the one doing most of the devouring. It's intense, endearing, and hilarious, all at the same time.

So...what makes Gomez and Morticia so rare...really?

How do I count the ways? These two have the *Art of Desire* DOWN.

1. They actually like and respect each other.
2. They hold the same values.
3. Verbal exchange is their very best form of foreplay.
4. This foreplay is an *all the time* habit, practiced inside and outside of the bedroom, keeping their blood running hot for each other and easily accessible.
5. They do more things *for* each other than *to* each other. They do things they know would please the other because they want their lover to be content.
6. It's clear that their sex life is off-the-charts. We know this because we ride their mental fantasies and repartee as they build sexual tension. They continue their connection *the next day* by acknowledging their primal lovemaking, each knowing how satisfied they are because of it. THIS IS IMPORTANT: With a beginning, middle, and end (foreplay, lovemaking, and acknowledgment), the end becomes the beginning, and the foreplay cycle continues. Gomez and Morticia keep their energetic bond flowing as their blood continues to circulate between the two of them at all times.

7. And finally, these ongoing verbal exchanges also make *other* possible mates boring to them, so the possibility of having an affair is essentially non-existent.

Even though Gomez and Morticia are fictional characters, their emotions and courting abilities are totally *doable*. Yes, high level, but learnable, as long as you have a partner you *like* (and they, you), and you hold the same life values.

Be sure to look up clips of Gomez and Morticia for a smile and a lesson.

QUESTIONS

1. What are your thoughts about the passion between Gomez and Morticia?
2. What about it do you like or not like?
3. Do they have something you'd like to emulate?

Twenty-Eight

The Gomez 2

We can not speak of Gomez without speaking of Gomez's *arm* kisses. There are 5 essential elements to Gomez's arm kisses.

1. When triggered by Morticia's intellectual conversation, sexual teasing, or French-speaking, he must express his passion.
2. He keeps it simple: He approaches either the interior of the arm or the posterior of the arm but never goes back and forth between the two. I've studied it.
3. He gets a good grasp on her arm. One hand holds her wrist and the other above her elbow. This controls where and how the kisses are placed.
4. He tastes and smells along the way if he can slow down long enough to do so!
5. No other woman (or arm) will do. He only has lips for

Morticia. More than anything, it's a mental game and attraction between these two.

The Technique

Posterior:

Beginning with the back of the hand, Gomez places ravenous and deliberate kisses and then continues up along the outside of Morticia's arm until he reaches the shoulder. He then repositions himself and continues kissing up to the neck, implementing "The Back-of-the-Neck Vampire," which we talked about in an earlier segment of *50 Kisses.* Or, instead of doing that kiss, he ventures down the center of her back. Ohhhh yeah.

Interior:

Gomez places his lips into the palm of Morticia's hand. He then moves to her wrist and proceeds to plant kisses along the inside of her arm until he reaches her armpit. It either stops there, or he continues up to her neck and engages in The Vampire (from the front). Fanning myself.

QUESTIONS

1. Have you ever tried "The Gomez 2?"
2. Do you have a special story about "The Gomez 2?"

Twenty-Nine

The Gomez 3

❦

Fingers. Gomez loves Morticia's. Gomez approaches the fingers in a similar way that he approaches the arm. Again, he sticks with a formula.

The Technique

Starting at the pinky, he kisses up the outside of the finger until he reaches the top and then dives into the interior side and web between fingers. Although it may look like he's chewing on chicken wings, he makes it clear that he is focused and enjoying every morsel. After covering each appendage, he moves on to the hand and nuzzles into it. "The Gomez 3" is a great stand-alone kiss or the starting point for an arm kiss.

Cara Mia!

Thirty

The Edge

W ant to send your loved one over the edge? This kiss isn't as much a kiss as an erotic experience for the ears. "The Edge" is a super easy thing to do, but there are quite a few essential things to consider.

The ear is a mecca for *pressure points* that relate to and heal various parts of the body (as well as conditions). It is both a sturdy and sensitive erogenous zone. So when you plan your pilgrimage to "The Edge," please go there knowing you are visiting sacred land.

Because of this, let's first cover what NOT to do. Let's go over SOUND. Being that the ear is a finely tuned sound receiver, any noise blasting into it not only hurts but could be damaging. You can't get reckless in the same way you can with other parts of the body. A slight sound goes a long way and is far louder to the Receiver than to the Lead. Mindfulness is the key here.

Things such as loud kissing, sloppy licking, darting tongue (See *The Dart* kiss), fingers poking around, and blowing air into the ear are unpleasant and generally come off as amplified irritation and ickiness. The goal is to provide something extraordinary.

The Technique

Almost anywhere on the outer portion of the ear feels good to massage. In this case, you'll merely be massaging small patches with your lips, tongue, and teeth.

Choose any part of the outer *edge* of the ear and place your lips on it. Begin to slowly suck and massage (with the lips) with as little noise or heavy breathing as possible. Gently bite down here and there, and sometimes even a little harder. Spend some time in each spot but don't overdo it. With your teeth, even pull on the whole ear without biting. Nibble and massage your way up or down the outer edge of the ear, repeating the process. Keep the experience relaxing. Not only do the nerve endings in the ear find this pleasant and sexually intoxicating, but the corresponding body parts that relate to the pressure points generally receive a slight wake-up call. Do you see where I'm going with this?

QUESTIONS

1. Have you ever had "The Edge" done on your ears?
2. What are your thoughts about "The Edge?"

Thirty-One

The Sloppy

"The Sloppy" is—you guessed it—a sloppy kiss. And, it's usually not a one-time thing. Instead, "The Sloppy" is generally delivered by an all-the-time sloppy kisser.

But a sloppy kisser doesn't necessarily mean a careless lover. It seems to me these folks just have a lot in common with bloodhounds. My observation is that their sense of smell is exceptionally high-tuned and they get all saliva-y when a love interest or a *potential* love interest enters their expanded field of sniffer-y.

"The Sloppy" kisser may drool all over the place, but they are the greatest of trackers and can pick up a scent in short order, giving their destination total focused attention. In other words, kissing may not be their best asset, but it doesn't mean they aren't great lovers in other areas.

So, I think "The Sloppy" kisser just might be someone who gets overexcited way too fast and needs to get from A-Z in a hurry. In this way, their mouth becomes a lubricating machine. This is fine if something needs lubricating, but the mouth and face usually do not.

However, despite the good lovin' otherwise or the sweet intention of the kisser (or the over-exuberance!), the actual "Sloppy" kiss part is not pleasant. It's kind of icky—actually, a lot icky.

So…if you've been told that you are a "Sloppy" kisser, then find a way to reign that in!

The Technique

While you're kissing, allow your tongue and flowing saliva juices to fly all over the place with no focus or regard for the person you're kissing. Not.

QUESTIONS

1. Have you ever tried "The Sloppy?"
2. What are your thoughts about "The Sloppy?"
3. Do you have a special story about "The Sloppy?"

Thirty-Two

The Picture

T his kiss should actually be called "The Kiss a Picture." Because that's what it is.

Now, before you feel ripped off that this simple kiss made the *50 Kisses* list, I want you to think about how often this kiss is used. How many times have you seen someone kiss their framed loved one in a movie or television show? In novels, how many times has a trenched war-torn soldier pulled a small, grubby picture out of his pocket while smoking a cigarette? Yearning for the comforts of home, he stares at his Beloved and kisses her before putting it away and returning to his wretched reality.

How often have you, yourself, looked at a picture of someone who has passed and kissed the person behind the glass (or mentally do it)? This loved one you are kissing might be a lover (past or present), a dear friend, child, parent, sibling, or cousin. Perhaps it's a remembrance of your favorite animal.

Since the beginning of sketched or photographed images, "The Picture" kiss has been at the top as one of the most "performed" kisses in history.

The Technique

Hold a photo (framed or not framed) or artistic likeness in your hand and contemplate the person you are viewing. Then, when feelings of heartfelt love arise, kiss the picture as a gesture of your connection, fondness, missing them, or blessing their journey.

QUESTIONS

1. Have you ever tried "The Picture?"
2. What are your thoughts about "The Picture?"
3. Do you have a special story about "The Picture?"

Thirty-Three

The Al Bacio

~~~⚬⚬⚬~~~

Not to be confused with "The Global" (or the Italian form of it, Il Bacio), "The Al Bacio" is one of those extraordinary kisses that only Italians can truly do right. Because, after all, part of the charm is that it represents generations upon generations of a passionate and vibrant culture within the person delivering the kiss.

So why do I add it to the *50 Kisses* list? Because it is too fantastic of a kiss not to acknowledge. I don't know of any other kiss or gesture that holds the same meaning to substitute it. The term "Chef's Kiss" is the term people have come to know, but *that's* known to be a made-up American marketing term created after WWll and doesn't give the respect the expression deserves.

"The Al Bacio" gesture is the highest of compliments meaning, "As good as a kiss." It's a kiss within a kiss.

"The Al Bacio" is used to express the sentiments of beauty, perfection, pleasure, appreciation, and magnificence while tipping its hat to "the kiss" as being the queen of all of these things.

The Technique

1. Pull the thumb and first two fingers together into a point.
2. Kiss the end of the point, then fling, with passion, the "as good as a kiss" message out into the air.

Here are my suggestions for using "The Al Bacio:"

1. If you're not Italian or it's not part of your natural upbringing or culture, just don't. Unless…
2. You need to "sign," and a thumbs-up just doesn't convey the required passion and magnificence.
3. You're writing an article and rating a movie, restaurant, performance, and so on. I've seen people use "Chef's Kiss!" While they're trying to give the highest compliment, it's a misuse. Instead, Use, "Al Bacio!" Honor the meaning and the culture. It's time to give appropriated practices back to the cultures that own them, no matter where one lives.

When used correctly in the right place at the right time and with the right passion, it's the only kiss that will do.

I never get tired of this gesture. It warms my heart and makes me smile. Look for samples online.

Thirty-Four

The Almost

"The Almost" is one of those kisses that *almost* happens in the movies to build up sexual tension.

It usually happens in one of two ways:

1. Two people find themselves in super close proximity of one another, and all of a sudden, realize that a kiss is about to (or could) happen. However, they know they shouldn't kiss for whatever reason, so resist! So harrowing!
2. The couple has been trying to get time to themselves, and when they finally do, they lean in for a kiss only to have someone walk into the room, which stops the kiss from happening.

The beauty of "The Almost" kiss is that it continues to build heated attraction until the lips finally meet at a future time.

The Technique

1. Faces get close, but lips never meet.

High drama torture!

QUESTIONS

1. Have you ever tried "The Almost?"
2. What are your thoughts about "The Almost?"
3. Do you have a memorable story about "The Almost?"

Thirty-Five

The Dip

~⚬୨୧⚬~

We all know what this one is. While it is easy to find "The Dip" in a dance, it is surprisingly hard to find good examples of dips for kissing online and in images.

"The Dip" is a classic move that everyone should learn and experience at least once!

The Technique

I'll outline the steps, and then you'll need to do them in one flowing move.

The Lead's role:
   This is better if you walk up and move right into it, but I'll give you the moves from a standing position:

- Facing your partner, position your feet about hip-distance apart for starters to have a solid and sturdy foundation.
- Reach around and place your right hand at the mid-back region of the Receiver's back and pull them into you.
- Do this while placing your left hand up high and behind the neck or top of back to balance your partner's weight and to know that you really "have" them. IMPORTANT! Where you place your left hand matters for proper posture and weight distribution for both of you. Most photos I see of "The Dip" don't have this aspect right.
- Anyhow, at the same time, take a decently sized step to the left and put your weight on your LEFT leg. The farther the step, the lower "The Dip."
- Bend the knee on that leg, and it will lower (dip) the Receiver. Keep your right foot on the floor.
- Allow your arms to hold your partner, but keep your poster straight to protect your back and keep you from dropping the Receiver.
- Now for the kiss: Pull your partner up to you while they are dipped back and lean down slightly to connect lips. Here's where you'll "plant" the perfect kiss.
- When finished, bring the Receiver all the way back up as you straighten your LEFT leg and shift your weight back to the center.

The RECEIVER's role:

- Place your hands on the Lead's shoulders or behind their neck.
- Once the Lead has their arms around your back and neck, *move your body with them* to your RIGHT.

- Slide your hands to a natural position to anchor yourself, but without pulling down on the Lead's neck.
- Put your weight on your RIGHT leg and bend your knee as the Lead starts to lower you.
- Twist your body slightly so that your back faces the floor and your front faces the ceiling.
- Allow your left leg to extend. Keep toes on the floor or allow your foot to lift slightly.
- Relax and let the Lead do their part.
- Participate in The Plant kiss when the Lead pulls your lips to theirs.
- Allow the Lead to pull you back up.
- Insert laughter or a knowing smile.

QUESTIONS

1. Have you ever tried "The Dip?"
2. What are your thoughts about "The Dip?"
3. Do you have a dramatic story about "The Dip?"

Thirty-Six

The Trace

A dangerously stretched-out "Almost" kiss added to "The Dip," I'm calling this seductive kiss, "The Trace."

This kiss traces a line from the cleavage to the tip of the chin (or in the reverse direction). It's an insanely hot addition to "The Dip" (standing, or dancing). Combine a few other kisses from the *50 Kisses* list (such as "The Back of the Neck Vampire," "The E-Zone," and "The Plant," and you've got the scene right out of the movie, *Frida*. Look this up online if you don't know it. If you're interested in seduction, this is the scene to watch.

The Technique

Whether standing or dancing, the Lead dips The Receiver (see "The Dip" kiss).

The LEAD's role:

You have two choices with "The Trace." Adjust your weight and hand placement to accommodate your choice, but either way, the Receiver's chest or neck must be arched ever-so-slightly in the process.

1. Nose and Lips: The Lead's nose and lips trace the path from The Receiver's cleavage to neck or lips without actually touching the skin, but tantalizingly close, smelling along the way.
2. Finger trace: The dip is less pronounced. The Lead's finger gently pushes the chin up and then, touching the skin, traces a line from there to the cleavage.

The RECEIVER's role:

Both versions allow the Lead to map it all out, so go with it. If the Lead touches a finger to your chin, lift your chin up—you are flowing with one another. This shouldn't be hard work for either of you.

Allow "The Trace" to be pure seduction.

QUESTIONS

1. Have you ever tried "The Trace?"
2. What are your thoughts about "The Trace?"
3. Do you have a tantalizing story about "The Trace?"

Thirty-Seven

The All-Encompassing

$$\sim\!\!\cdot\!\!\infty\!\!\cdot\!\!\sim$$

"The All-Encompassing" kiss is probably only experienced by people with small mouths, thin lips, or both. However, *the lesson* can be received by anyone willing to go beyond their boundaries to move big or small obstacles in any situation; to *find a way* rather than say, "It can't be done"; to break free of control to problem-solve.

Rather than fun or steamy, this is a rebel kiss that takes a total departure from our *50 Kisses* lineup and instead delivers an existential journey into significant personal growth and expansion, yet it's still a kiss. The lessons I gained from this kiss would later serve and assist me in business and other areas of challenge in my life.

Yes, kisses can do that.

So if this doesn't sound like your thing, you might want to skip to the next kiss.

But if curious, read on...

While my lips are on the thinner side, my mouth size is average, as far as I know. I hadn't really thought about it until a meeting of the minds, and a hefty dose of animal magnetism took the reigns at a multi-day event I attended with friends and friends of friends.

In contrast to mine, he had both an enormous mouth and big beautiful lips. As he swooped in for the kiss, his mouth *completely* engulfed mine. I didn't expect that. His lips covered the entire outside of my mouth! I cannot say it was unpleasant, just strange but a bit erotic too, as if I was being overtaken by some other-worldly creature who smelled and tasted amazing. Even so, *he* didn't seem to notice (or care about) the disparity, so if I were going to be part of this exchange and genuinely enjoy myself, *I* would need to be the one to adjust to meet his "Lip Lock."

Sizing up the situation immediately, I knew I could buy myself time by getting down to pleasurable work with several of the kisses in my "French Kiss" toolbox. The problem is that *that* plan would be a mental job, and my goal was to get out of my head. Therefore, I would still need to loosen up and expand my mouth's reach to be more comfortable.

Alchemy was in order. Transmutation.

After quickly evaluating my options one more time, my only choice and the only thing left to do was to trust in the surrendering of my *everything*: my personal control of the situation and the self-control of my being.

Even though I recognize this sounds totally extreme and dramatic and possibly (probably) weird, at the time, I didn't want to over-think it or think about it at all. I was already on the way to outer space and just wanted to keep going with this beautiful and cool person without interruption or getting hung up. He was delivering a slow, smooth, and dreamy ride, and I wanted to stay on board. So…I visualized relaxing fully, allowing myself to release my jaw (as best as that seems possible), and then release a bit more with each breath to open up completely, to become *unhinged* to meet another.

My lips found their way to his, meeting fully, and in the surrender, I *did* let go of everything—of it all. I let go of my identity and began to slip; to sink in; to fall into the abyss and receive; to allow; to float on top of rocking, hypnotic waters; to experience timelessness and weightlessness; to feel and not feel; to be a part of; to disappear into Oneness.

Many years later, I learned something important that made it all make sense: That our jaws are structural pillars of our power. They are an area of the body responsible for keeping our acts together. The jaw is stoic—a shield that maintains the person's integrity. It is a primal protector—ready to fight and clamp down on anything that threatens to hurt us. It chews our food into nutrition that maintains our strength and health.

Anatomically, the entire body relaxes when the jaw relaxes, especially the womb area. It is a trick of smoother childbirth. The very practice of blowing during labor is a deliberate act of relaxing the jaw, releasing oxytocin (the trust and bonding hormone), and relaxing the uterus and cervix so that mother and child may navigate the passage successfully transcending the veils of spirit. This ability of our amazing bodies is there for us when needed.

Let go. Relax the jaw. Surrender. Trust. Unhinge. Allow. Receive. Feel. Float.

In the acceptance, I had let go of all past, present, and future stresses; of image and ego and boundaries and shoulds and should nots. I was Free. I was *present* (and not present). I was Joy. I was Bliss.

Yes, Bliss.

All-Encompassing Bliss. And all from the All-Encompassing kiss.

QUESTIONS

1. Have you experienced something similar to "The All-Encompassing?"
2. What are your thoughts about "The All-Encompassing?"
3. Do you have a transformation story from a kissing experience?

Thirty-Eight

The Sherlock

A lso affectionately called "The Sherlolly" because of the characters Sherlock and Molly, this kiss comes flying straight through the window from the series *Sherlock*.

"The Sherlock" kiss is "The Plant" on steroids. I will try, but I honestly can't do this kiss justice by describing it, so please look up the Sherlolly Kiss or the episode called *The Empty Hearse*. Watch, enjoy, and learn.

The Technique

While I don't suggest swinging on a rope and crashing through a window to kiss your love interest, you could certainly try this:

When going from one place to another, enter and walk quickly through a room and find your target (the Receiver). Take them by surprise by marching right up to them while shaking off your coat and straightening out your hair from the action-packed walk. Pause and take a breath to focus on your sweetheart, then bring your hands down to cup both sides of the head at the jaw. Position the face and "Plant" *The Perfect Kiss*.

Let time standstill.

Release, and proceed out the door to wherever you are going.

True story (I have witnesses): I actually had a version of this happen to me. I was waiting in a big open area with friends to get into an event. I heard my name called out. I turned around just in time to watch a bicyclist, helmet and all, ride right up to me and stop, put his hands on the sides of my head, tilt it, and land "The Plant" on me! Then he smiled and rode off, telling me to have a great day!

I did after that. And *that's* "The Sherlock" kiss!

QUESTIONS

1. Have you ever tried "The Sherlock?"
2. What are your thoughts about "The Sherlock?"
3. Do you have a surprising story about "The Sherlock?"

Thirty-Nine

The Whip

~ ‿◦‿ ~

No, this is a different type of whip. "The Whip" kiss is a tasty treat, as in "whipped cream." You all know the drill on this one. Put whipped cream anywhere on your sweetie and eat, lick, or kiss it off.

The various versions of this kiss are just as delectable!

The Technique

1. **"The Whip"**: Put whipped cream anywhere you like on your Sweetie. Then proceed to eat, lick, or slurp it off. "French Kiss" the area to make sure you clean your plate.
2. **"The Chocolate"**: Get super fancy by laying down some chocolate, then add whipped cream on top of it. Chocolate is one of those things that can be finger-painted or brushed on. Choose the chocolate bar of your choice (since you'll

be the one licking it off) and melt it down. Allow it to cool enough to begin applying to your sweetie's body. Create a work of art in an area (basic or extensive), and then lick off to your heart's content. Follow this by an extended "French Kiss" of the site since chocolate is more challenging to remove than whipped cream!

3. "**The Wedding Cake**": This is a little more like "The Lady and the Tramp" kiss, where food is the reason for lips-to-lips contact. There's a right way and a wrong way to do this one unless both people are in complete agreement that the wrong way is the right way. First, the couple needs to cut the wedding cake.

- *The wrong way* is to smash the wedding cake all over the bride or groom's face. Not cool, especially for the bride who has most likely spent a fortune having her hair and makeup done.
- *The right way* is to feed the cake to each other simultaneously, making it into the mouth, with a gentle smashing of it around the lips. They kiss with whipped cream-caked lips. A particularly nice touch is to wipe some of it off the other's lip with your finger to taste it. Of course, by this time of the reception, the bride probably has to fix her lipstick anyhow.

And then they dance.

QUESTION

1. Do you have a special story about "The Whip?"

Forty

The Conversation

"**T**he Conversation" is my favorite kiss of all because it is, in my opinion, the most intimate of all. And I think it is the most intimate of all because you can't fake it. You can't do this with just anyone.

It is, in so many ways, the moment of truth.

But it doesn't mean that the person you're doing this with is your "forever" person or partner. However, if you have a partner, this kiss would not be something you'd do with someone else (depending on the rules of your partnership). It's GP+ rated but highly personal. And just to be clear, this might *not* be a kiss you could actually do with your committed partner if something significant is missing in your relationship. Two people just have to have something special between them for this to be wonderful.

92

Chemistry and an unspoken trust are needed.

I say this because the person I learned "The Conversation" kiss from was not a beau, but instead, a friend who was casually sweet on me and me, him. Neither was interested in a relationship, but we liked being affectionate when the opportunity presented itself. We had an understanding—and that special something between us that worked for this kind of thing.

The Technique

I'll share this technique by telling the way it happened.

1. It was always a surprise and a pleasure to run into him. We'd say hello with a friendly full-body hug.
2. From the hug, his *forehead* (and possibly) nose would find mine. Comfortably pressed together, a deep breath was taken. It was the acknowledgment of a sacred coming-together—a ceremonial gesture done in the same way that a martial arts student bows to their opponent.
3. With this forehead gesture, it's important not to confuse or disrespect the deep and rich cultural meanings of the Maori Hongi or the Hawaiian Honi (forehead-/nose/breath) greetings. However, the forehead-pressing of this kiss *does* share some of the same qualities. Your faces are touching, and you're sharing breath. Wisdom and respect are being acknowledged. Something ancient and grounded is going on.
4. However, the forehead exchange I'm explaining is also sensual, which makes it very different from those greetings,

which are *not*.

5. Next, a low-voiced conversation would begin. Yes, a conversation.

6. Catching up on what we had been up to and giving compliments of attraction, our heads would naturally move when ready and slowly tilt to line up cheeks or nose. Sweet *Planted* kisses on the lips happened in between—sometimes even as one of us talked. Often, opposite sides of the face would line up, and we'd then speak into each other's ear. Kisses would happen there too. Just to be clear, this isn't a "French Kiss" make-out session and robust expression of passion. Hands rest on shoulders or behind the neck. If doing this in public, no one is yelling, "Get a room!" but no one will interrupt you either, since it is obvious you're engaged in your own private conversation.

7. When warm and dizzy from accelerated heartbeats and breathing, we'd reluctantly complete our time together and say goodbye.

At this juncture, for anyone trying "The Conversation," a decision must be made about what to do next. Go home or continue someplace in private?

QUESTIONS

1. Have you ever tried "The Conversation?"
2. What are your thoughts about "The Conversation?"
3. Do you have a seductive story about "The Conversation?"

Forty-One

The Outlander

~⚬⚬~

"I want ye so much I can scarcely breathe."

I call this kiss "The Outlander" because it is the way Jamie Fraser, the hunky Scottish lead in the episodic show (based on Diane Gabaldon's book series), approached, maybe not all, but most of his kisses (from what I can tell).

While the show isn't everyone's Scotch whiskey, *Outlander* is a must-watch for improving one's romantic and relationship know-how. There is a reason the lead couple has hot sex. Even though they have different ways of going about it, they have a lot in common with Gomez and Morticia Addams (#27, 28, 29). They simply have much more between them than sexual physicality—their emotional foreplay is ongoing. This sets them up for the intimacy required for this kiss.

The Technique

"The Outlander" kiss is *an approach* that could (and should) be learned by anyone to upgrade their kissing mindset. While it takes a bit of practice to get its finesse, it's an excellent skill to have for *any* day and for *any* kiss.

When I first saw Jamie Fraser's kiss, I recognized it as familiar. It took me a while to figure out what it was because it's got something in common, yet different, from a kiss I experienced—"The Conversation." In the case of "The Outlander," it's not about quietly speaking with heads together (even though at times, Jamie Fraser does that too); instead, there's a **highly subtle** tilt that happens as he leans in for a kiss— he *leads* with his forehead (or sometimes cheek) and lets that touch the Receiver's face before planting the kiss. This anchors the kiss and connects the two people before lips touch. The difference between the two kisses is that "The Conversation" never gets into "make out" mode, while "The Outlander" is all about making out after the kiss gets started.

I want to clarify that he isn't ramming his head into hers! This move is barely there but powerful. You have to watch it a few times to catch it, but it makes a difference.

1. He looks into his partner's eyes,
2. then deliberately *positions his body* (while heavy breathing increases by both),
3. then leans in for the kiss with his forehead first (ever so slightly), touching hers (barely)
4. and rolls his head to plant the kiss.

The method grounds the two people together before the kiss happens, and it's a non-threatening take-charge-of-the-kiss move. It all happens in one smooth motion, but that *one* action is a torrid bodice-ripper, no matter the century.

QUESTION

1. What are your thoughts about "The Outlander" approach?
2. Have you tried it?
3. Do you have a steamy story about "The Outlander?"
4. If you watch the series, what else do you love about the kissing (and everything else) that goes on?

Forty-Two

The Talk-to-Me

I didn't think anything about "The Talk-to-Me" until a girlfriend of mine confided in me that sex with her husband was functionally fantastic but empty. The problem? He wouldn't talk to her or make any noise before, during, or after sex, which she desired. She was unhappy.

When she communicated with him that she would love some participation or communication during their intimate time together, he thought it was a silly request and did not attempt to satisfy her appeal. Needless to say, the marriage didn't last.

Of course, the reason for the conflict wasn't because he wasn't a talker, but because he wouldn't try the one intimate thing that she was asking for and was vital to her. After a while, a person loses interest, or worse, begins to lose their personal life force when they don't feel valued by their partner—when that partner refuses to take the request seriously or make an effort.

If either of you is asking for something that could be physically or emotionally painful, then that's another story and should be communicated. But if the request is reasonable and you love this person, then giving it a try shouldn't be a hardship but rather an opportunity to keep your love alive. There comes a time when you need to evaluate whether you feel valued or if *you* value your partner (and relationship) enough to make an effort to meet the other's needs. Perhaps each values the other, but your patterns and ways don't line up.

She was after intimacy in presence and breath as well as sexual physicality. She wanted to participate with someone, not just be a body in the bed or a person that makes dinner. He needed someone who didn't need that or see it that way.

The Technique

Intimacy and foreplay come in many packages. It's best if these things can be present inside *and* outside the bedroom. One thing is for sure: It has to happen somewhere and consistently for a love relationship to last.

Outside of the bedroom would include working together as a team to create your lifestyle and allow both peoples' dreams to come true. Intimacy is about *liking* and enjoying each other's company—wanting the best for both and honoring each's requests when possible. When this happens, intimacy within the bedroom is far more heightened and sweet.

There is great power in verbal exchanges. It can be a powerful aphrodisiac to "pillow talk"—to share thoughts and feelings as confidantes. I know a few people who read to one another, which provides comfort, security, and a sense of belonging. When making love, hearing pleasure coming out of your loved one's mouth, whether in sounds or words, tells you they are present and with you and don't want to be anywhere else.

Sexuality makes everyone vulnerable, so even the slightest exchange can be enormously affirming. The deeper the groans, moans, or words, the more erotically it vibrates within the lower parts of the body. Afterward, smiles or accolades and spooning up can carry your relationship a long way.

If you or your sweetheart aren't natural talkers, it doesn't really matter. What *does* matter is that intimacy is communicated throughout the day or night *somehow*. This way, responses during physically intimate times aren't missed. The key is for it to be authentic.

QUESTIONS

1. What are your thoughts about "The Talk-to-Me?"
2. Do you have an experience with "The Talk-to-Me?"

Forty-Three

The Tasty

~ ⟨୧୨୭⟩ ~

"The Tasty" kiss is a *series* of kisses ending with a deliberate kiss sound. It tastes and sounds delicious. It's a sweet kiss to do on the other side of hurried passion, or perhaps when lounging around on a picket blanket near a lake. It is somewhat of a sleepy kiss.

The Technique

"The Tasty" is a lusciously delivered series of deliberate "Plant" kisses. The difference with this kiss, as opposed to "The Plant" kiss by itself, is that this isn't just one kiss, but many, and it is more satisfying than intoxicating.

1. The Lead delivers one "Plant" kiss after another—slowly paced—each ending with a no-mistaking "tasting kiss noise" as you release.

2. The Sound: When ending the kiss, pull the sealed lips together a bit more (yet keeping them soft) before you release with a sort of "muah" thing. But it's the lips that make the sound, not your vocal cords. It's slightly too loud (too much kissing TMI) for public consumption but sweet and satisfying medicine to the ears in private.

QUESTIONS

1. Have you ever tried "The Tasty?"
2. What are your thoughts about "The Tasty?"
3. 3) Do you have a delicious story about "The Tasty?"

Forty-Four

The Butterfly

"The Butterfly" kiss is just one of those dang cute kisses meant to surprise and delight the other person. Adult or kid, it's a fun and somewhat ticklish bit of affection.

The Technique

1. "The Butterfly" kiss is done with the eyelashes! Place your face up close to someone's cheek. Gently press the bones of your eye socket onto their skin and flutter your lashes.
2. Adjust according to the length of your lashes. The idea is to flutter them quickly and easily. The Butterfly can be done anywhere on the body.

The shoulder is a fun target to sneak up on.

Forty-Five

The Lipstick

"The Lipstick" kiss is the one you'll find yourself either wiping off or keeping, depending on who's lips were pressed to your cheek.

A lipstick print is SO much hotter than smoking cigarettes or donning a hickey.

My friends, Moriah and Jedediah, actually made this mark permanent. Jed wanted Moriah's lips tattooed onto his neck, so they made a lipstick print of her lips. They took it to his tattoo artist who copied the image, put ink to neck, and completed the job! It's one of the best tatts I've seen. I love it.

But you **don't** need to get a tattoo to have a set of lips (temporarily) fixed to your skin!

The Technique

Whoever will be wearing the lipstick print:

1. Decide where you want the lipstick print to go—neck, cheek, forehead, or anywhere else you'd like to place a kiss.
2. Choose clothes to wear that will make the print visible. In addition, you won't want the clothes to smear the print *or* the print to mess up the clothes!

Whoever is going to deliver the kiss:

1. Cover the lips with a nice, even layer of lipstick—not too thick and not too thin. Make sure all edges are covered.
2. Blot lightly with tissue to get an overabundance of lipstick off, but leave enough to make a print. Practice a few times on your hand to try it out, and then reapply the lipstick and blot again if you think it needs it.
3. Know that you'll need to be deliberate about placing the kiss so that you don't mush the lips around and get a blurred print. The good news is, if you mess up, you can clean it off with soap and water and start over. However, it's good to get it right the first time so that you're not leaving a red area from rubbing it off or stain from the lipstick.
4. When ready, go for it. *Plant* a kiss with the right amount of pressure. Voila! Have fun!

To keep the lipstick print from smudging, try giving it a quick dusting with a translucent powder.

QUESTIONS

1. Have you ever had a lipstick print?
2. Do you have a fun story about "The Lipstick?"
3. Do you have a lipstick print tattoo?

Give yourself some love! Practice and put some of your lipstick prints all over this page. Be sure to blot first!

Forty-Six

The Anatomy Class

❦

One of the sexiest kisses of them all is what I call "The Anatomy Class" kiss.

At the time, my husband was teaching Anatomy and Physiology. He liked to stay sharp, so I got to be on the receiving end of his practice sessions. I'm pretty sure he came up with this kissing approach on the spot one night. Lucky me! I also enjoyed being woken up by it. Anytime is divine...

You now get to benefit too.

"The Anatomy Class" kiss is a game of blending knowledge and sensual giving by the Lead and an over-the-top liquefying experience for the Receiver. It can arouse—or cause someone to fall into a deep, healing sleep, depending on when it is done and the energy levels and intentions of Lead and Receiver.

Everyone can do this. Here are my recommendations for your anatomy knowledge level:

- If you're a **human anatomy expert or student**, do your best to stick with the Greek or Latin terms, as this is what adds to the sex appeal of this kissing session (and it really *will* help you to remember the terminology!). Remember, the brain is the largest sex organ in the body. Not only does this activity deliver pleasure beyond measure, but intelligence is a bonus attraction.

- If you're **neither of the above** regarding anatomy knowledge, the bonus attraction comes in the form of "wanting to give pleasure, being game, and having fun." That's always a plus in a partner. Your loved one will appreciate your enthusiasm and desire. Achieve the same erotic results by identifying body parts and areas with plain ol' English or whatever language you naturally speak.

...which leads me to think of more ways to deliver the experience:

- **Use another language**. If your *poa only speaks English, but you also speak Spanish, then by all means, identify body parts in your sexiest Español.

- **Try an accent or character**: You could also deliver this experience by naming parts in your best Scottish, Southern, or Caribbean accent. Or perhaps you could play a polite, deep-voiced cowboy or seductive wench.

- **Give the parts new names** when you want to: Instead of the hip bone, it might be called "my favorite spot" or whatever. This one might take more creative brainpower than you have at the moment, but it could be used to highlight your places of interest (you get the idea). There are as many choices as your imagination can conjure, so there is no excuse to not give this fantastic activity a try!

The Technique

The Lead: This sensual experience is meant to flow organically and without stress. In other words, don't try too hard. Enjoy your loved one's body and whisper your way through the process, or use a low, relaxed volume.

The Receiver: Lie down in bed (or someplace comfortable), either face up or down. The temperature of the room must be just right.

The Lead can begin anywhere on the body. Here are **two suggestions to choose from for starting:**

1. Begin by naturally **kissing** the Receiver on the lips and talking a bit. When ready, kiss again and name the lips, either by whispering "lips" or by the anatomical name, *labia oris*. If you want to really get into it, you could name upper and lower lips and the tongue, etc. Or skip that altogether, move on to the cheek, jaw, or brows and go from there.

2. Begin by **stroking the skin or lightly massaging** any body area that is not a private part. The idea is for this to be a sensuous and luxurious experience. When ready, position yourself to lay your lips on the first body part to be named.

The General Rules of the Game: Each time you land on an area of interest, *Plant* your nicest firm*, but soft kiss, then come up for air and quietly announce that particular body part's correct anatomical name (or the familiar name). Then, continue to the next location of choice.

*I say "firm" because you're kissing pressure points all over the body. While you want your lips to be relaxed and soft, you also want the kiss to make a healing impact, as if giving a pressure point massage with your mouth. So press in a bit.

Move slowly, rhythmically, and methodically around the entire body (the longer the linger, the better). The idea is to admire and scientifically identify as many places on the body as possible without making mistakes. If an error is made, the Lead will need to repeat the gesture, staying there and kissing until the term is remembered (darn!). Another thing that can happen is temporary amnesia. If the Lead lands on a particularly fine patch of land that causes them to lose focus and memory, forgetting the anatomical name, they may choose to stay there longer, give the part a name of their own choosing, or vow to come back to this spot at another time.

BONUS POINTS: Gentle bites or sucking can be substituted for kisses or blended into the mix as an alternative option.

Finishing: Once the trip around the Receiver's landscape is complete, allow the Receiver's state to dictate the following actions. Is luxuriating in each other's arms and falling asleep the course, or is the Receiver feeling energetic and impassioned? Go from there.

I suggest switching roles and reciprocating with The Anatomy Class at another time. The Receiver MUST be allowed to fully receive without mustering the energy to reciprocate after their session is complete.

QUESTIONS

1. Have you ever tried "The Anatomy Class?"
2. What are your thoughts about "The Anatomy Class?"
3. Do you have a sensuous story about "The Anatomy Class?"

*person of affection

Forty-Seven

The Dragon's Kiss

O ur next sizzler is called "The Dragon's Kiss" for a reason. When taken by surprise, this kiss will rise up, singe your lips, and shoot flaming blue fire through your privates if you're not careful.

Not that that's a bad thing.

This true story comes from my gal pal, Lulu.

You see, he was waiting for her in the hallway when she got home from work. They were long-lost loves who hadn't seen each other in too many years. She called him "Dragon" because he's *smokin' hot* (and other reasons she cleverly refused to divulge). Standing there, wearing his green silk robe, he smiled that smile—that smile that always did it whether she wanted it to or not. That smile that always ignited her inferno—the one that *this time* had been dormant for what felt like an eternity.

She knew he would show up at some point, but the arrival time was unclear. The train had been delayed due to snow on the tracks, and worsening weather was predicted. Despite all that, here he was.

Finally.

Walking toward him, she first dropped her purse to the floor, then keys, followed by her coat. She kicked off her shoes.

She knew she had to slow time down, take a forever picture in her mind, and enjoy the moment. Who knows how long it would be until they saw each other again? She'd need immediate self-control. Every cell in her body felt charged and electrified; every heartbeat threw sparks.

That smile. Those lips. And whatever was *not underneath* the green silk robe that Dragon was still wearing.

She moved closer and closer, as if in a slow-motion movie scene until her lips were a hair's breadth from his. She could feel his breathing. She inhaled his masculinity. He watched, amused. He wanted her, but he waited. And yet, she did not touch. He knew to stay still.

They had done this before.

And then she began. Lulu lit the match by barely touching his lips with hers. Accepting the torch, Dragon's heat took over to

113

stoke the fire, taking her in his arms and *Planting* the perfect kiss as steam escaped all fingers and toes, fully engulfing them in a blaze of passion.

Spark ~ Ignite ~ Engulf. In that order.

"The Dragon's Kiss" is the ultimate, swoon-worthy romance-novel-kiss—a combination of *The Almost*, *The Vampire*, *The Plant*, and the *Lip Lock*—whose memory will keep you smoldering forevermore.

HOT, HOT, HOT!

QUESTIONS

1. Have you ever tried "The Dragon's Kiss?"
2. Do you have a Dragon in your life?
3. Do you have a smokin' hot story about "The Dragon's Kiss?"

Forty-Eight

The Exo-Exo

⟨∘⟩

"The Exo-Exo" kiss is this one: XOXO, which means "hugs and kisses."

But…which is the hug and which is the kiss? The hug is the O because you're encircling each other, wrapping around the other. The kiss is the X because it represents lips coming together between you. OR…is it the other way around? With the X representing two people embracing and the O meaning the joining (opened) mouths? There seem to be many opinions about this one, so you decide. Either way, "The Exo-Exo" is considered a lighthearted "hugs and kisses" gesture between friends, families, and lovers.

QUESTION

1. Was your "Exo-Exo" ever misunderstood?

115

Forty-Nine

The Marilyn

꧁ ❀ ꧂

W ho doesn't love her or this kiss? "The Marilyn" is a big fat double "MUAAAH!"

However, there are many versions of the "MUAAAH!" and just as many names and varying intentions. It is sometimes referred to as The Air Kiss, The Flying Kiss, or the I Love You and Goodnight Everyone! kiss, among others.

Marilyn's version was different than the rest though. Her kiss was *a two-kiss* kiss.

While this two-step kiss by any set of names obviously sends love to anyone in its path, there is one kiss that it is not: this is NOT *blowing a kiss*. "The Blow a Kiss" is much more distinct. We'll talk about that in the following *50 Kisses* kiss!

The Technique

"The Marilyn" kiss:

1. Begin by covering your mouth with your *whole* hand and kissing the inside middle of your hand, then swing it back out to "throw the kiss."
2. Follow this up with another kiss without the hand. This time, look at your target and make the kissing motion. (Air Kiss).

Michael Jackson's version:

1. Kiss fingers on one hand and swing the arm out from left to right (or right to left) to spread the kiss across the crowd.

Mr. Paradise's version (I love this personal expression of love):

1. He kisses the fingers and then hands the kiss straight to you. And to me. Sweet.

Suggestion: Look these GIFs up online. It's better when you see them.

QUESTIONS

1. Have you ever tried "The Marilyn?"
2. What version of this kiss do you prefer?

Fifty

The Blow a Kiss

So here we are. NUMBER 50, which is "The Blow a Kiss!"

It wasn't until I was researching this particular kiss, looking for examples, did I discover how many people *think* they are blowing a kiss but aren't! I found very few examples of people doing "The Blow a Kiss" correctly. At least in my picky opinion (but look it up for yourself).

The last kiss we talked about, "The Marilyn," is a THROWN kiss with various ways to do it. Those kisses do not actually get BLOWN to someone. However, they *do* direct the kiss *with their hand* (or mouth) to one or more people. They are throwing a kiss, not blowing a kiss. See the difference?

When searching online, decide whether someone is throwing or blowing a kiss. Or neither!

The Technique

The Blow a Kiss is a smooth three-stepper:

1. Kiss your hand.
2. Then lay that hand *flat*, just under chin-to-shoulder height.
3. …and deliberately blow the kiss you just put into your hand, to someone or everyone.

It can be done with one or both hands.

Here are some perfect examples of "The Blow a Kiss." Please search for these GIFS as it's better to see this kiss in action. Specifically, look up these folks who do the kiss correctly:

1. Piper Perabo
2. Mixed martial artist, CM Punk
3. Rachel McAdams blowing a kiss in the movie "Mean Girls."
4. And my very favorite, Cary Elwes in *Robin Hood, Men in Tights*. Here, you'll also see someone *catching* the kiss.

Too much fun.

QUESTIONS

1. Have you been "Blowing a Kiss" correctly?
2. Have you ever caught a blown kiss?
3. Do you have a special story about "The Blow a Kiss?"

Kissing Counts

The next few pages are designed for you to count your kisses!

1. Mark (check off) what you've tried and the date if you like
2. Rate them on a scale of 1 - 10, with 10 being the highest.
3. What did you like or not like?
4. How did you improve this kiss?
5. Make any notes that might be helpful for next time or for the reason of just wanting to remember the experience!
6. Get creative! Draw, color, paste pics, or leave lipstick prints.

FIRST KISS: Done _____ Date: _____
    Rating: _____ Notes:

.

THE PLANT: Done _____ Date: _____
  Rating: _____ Notes:

THE LIP LINER: Done _____ Date: _____
  Rating: _____ Notes:

THE WRAPPER: Done _____ Date: _____
  Rating: _____ Notes:

THE NIPPER: Done _____ Date: _____
  Rating: _____ Notes:

THE POP: Done _____ Date: _____
  Rating: _____ Notes:

.

THE VAMPIRE: Done _____ Date: _____
  Rating: _____ Notes:

THE BACK—OF-THE-NECK VAMPIRE: Done _____
  Date: _____ Rating: _____ Notes:

THE VAMPIRATE: Done _____ Date: _____
  Rating: _____ Notes:

THE HICKEY: Done _____ Date: _____
  Rating: _____ Notes:

THE PURSE: Done _____ Date: _____
  Rating: _____ Notes:

.

THE PEPPERMINT: Done _____ Date: _____
    Rating: _____ Notes:

THE HOT: Done _____ Date: _____
    Rating: _____ Notes:

THE BONES: Done _____ Date: _____
    Rating: _____ Notes:

THE LADY AND THE TRAMP: Done _____ Date: _____
    Rating: _____ Notes:

THE GLOBAL: Done _____ Date: _____
    Rating: _____ Notes:

.

THE NICE-TO-SEE-YOU: Done _____ Date: _____
  Rating: _____ Notes:

THE HOLLYWOOD: Done _____ Date: _____
  Rating: _____ Notes:

THE GIVER AND THE RECEIVER: Done _____
  Date: _____ Rating: _____ Notes:

THE TUG - HAIR: Done _____ Date: _____
  Rating: _____ Notes:

THE TUG - BEARD: Done _____ Date: _____
  Rating: _____ Notes:

.

THE MUZZLE NUZZLE: Done _____ Date: _____
  Rating: _____ Notes:

The E-ZONE: Done _____ Date: _____
  Rating: _____ Notes:

THE DART: Done _____ Date: _____
  Rating: _____ Notes:

THE TONGUE-in-CHEEK: Done _____ Date: _____
  Rating: _____ Notes:

THE GOMEZ 1: Done _____ Date: _____
  Rating: _____ Notes:

.

THE GOMEZ 2: Done _____ Date: _____
    Rating: _____ Notes:

THE GOMEZ 3: Done _____ Date: _____
    Rating: _____ Notes:

THE EDGE: Done _____ Date: _____
    Rating: _____ Notes:

THE SLOPPY: Done _____ Date: _____
    Rating: _____ Notes:

THE PICTURE: Done _____ Date: _____
    Rating: _____ Notes:

.

THE AL BACIO: Done _____ Date: _____
   Rating: _____ Notes:

THE ALMOST: Done _____ Date: _____
   Rating: _____ Notes:

THE DIP: Done _____ Date: _____
   Rating: _____ Notes:

THE TRACE: Done _____ Date: _____
   Rating: _____ Notes:

THE ALL-ENCOMPASSING: Done _____ Date: _____
   Rating: _____ Notes:

.

THE SHERLOCK: Done _____ Date: _____
  Rating: _____ Notes:

THE WHIP: Done _____ Date: _____
  Rating: _____ Notes:

THE CONVERSATION: Done _____ Date: _____
  Rating: _____ Notes:

THE OUTLANDER: Done _____ Date: _____
  Rating: _____ Notes:

THE TALK-TO-ME: Done _____ Date: _____
  Rating: _____ Notes:

.

THE TASTY: Done _____ Date: _____
  Rating: _____ Notes:

THE BUTTERFLY: Done _____ Date: _____
  Rating: _____ Notes:

THE LIPSTICK: Done _____ Date: _____
  Rating: _____ Notes:

THE ANATOMY CLASS: Done _____ Date: _____
  Rating: _____ Notes:

THE DRAGON'S KISS: Done _____ Date: _____
  Rating: _____ Notes:

.

THE EXO-EXO: Done _____ Date: _____
   Rating: _____ Notes:

THE MARILYN: Done _____ Date: _____
   Rating: _____ Notes:

The Blow a Kiss: Done _____ Date: _____
   Rating: _____ Notes:

Final Thoughts:

Love and Thanks

Thank you so much for taking a spin through this book. Did you try any of the kisses? What is your favorite? What kiss did I leave out?

As I suggested in the "Introduction," perhaps try a different kiss every day for ten days. If it works out to be a spicy adventure, then keep going!

In addition, I hope I've inspired you to observe kissing in movies and episodic shows. When you come across an arousing kiss, take note. Did you learn anything that you'd like to try? Did you notice anything that you want to be sure *not* to do?

I'll leave you with these lyrics from the song, "Kiss" by *Prince and The Revolution* and a suggestion to search for the official music video from 1986. He nails mature seduction mixed with ridiculous fun (and finally gets the girl). PLUS, there's a quick and effective "Back-of-the-Neck Vampire" and a fantastic "Shoulder Vampire" as a bonus at the very end! I love that!

...

You don't have to be rich
To be my girl
You don't have to be cool
To rule my world
Ain't no particular sign
I'm more compatible with
I just want your extra time and your...
Kiss

Love and thanks,
  Sym

Reviews

Reviews assist other readers to find books that might be of benefit to them. Reviews also help Indie authors and publishers (like me) to be found online. If you like this book, I'd appreciate it if you'd take a moment to leave a good review on your favorite review site such as Goodreads or Amazon.

Thank you!

About the Author

Sym Scott has been observing, researching, and experimenting with kissing since the 2nd grade after witnessing a breathtaking lip-lock by a couple standing in line at a baseball game.

Vowing to have one (or many) of those kisses someday, Sym began noticing the nuances of kisses in movies and television. From there, collating and publishing the kisses collected along the way (whether observed or personally practiced) seemed like the logical next step and the right thing to do for the good of the planet. Personal favorites are kisses #46, 38, and 28, with a bonus round of #10.

Sym lives in the Pacific Northwest, a kissing haven with great music, ecotherapy, and pretty good donuts.

Made in the USA
Monee, IL
12 June 2024

59793142R00085